Appalachian Fiddler
Albert Hash

Contributions to Southern Appalachian Studies

1. *Memoirs of Grassy Creek: Growing Up in the Mountains on the Virginia–North Carolina Line.* Zetta Barker Hamby. 1998
2. *The Pond Mountain Chronicle: Self-Portrait of a Southern Appalachian Community.* Edited by Leland R. Cooper and Mary Lee Cooper. 1998
3. *Traditional Musicians of the Central Blue Ridge: Old Time, Early Country, Folk and Bluegrass Label Recording Artists, with Discographies.* Marty McGee. 2000
4. *W.R. Trivett, Appalachian Pictureman: Photographs of a Bygone Time.* Ralph E. Lentz II. 2001
5. *The People of the New River: Oral Histories from the Ashe, Alleghany and Watauga Counties of North Carolina.* Edited by Leland R. Cooper and Mary Lee Cooper. 2001
6. *John Fox, Jr., Appalachian Author.* Bill York. 2003
7. *The Thistle and the Brier: Historical Links and Cultural Parallels Between Scotland and Appalachia.* Richard Blaustein. 2003
8. *Tales from Sacred Wind: Coming of Age in Appalachia. The Cratis Williams Chronicles.* Cratis D. Williams. Edited by David Cratis Williams and Patricia D. Beaver. 2003
9. *Willard Gayheart, Appalachian Artist.* Willard Gayheart and Donia S. Eley. 2003
10. *The Forest City Lynching of 1900: Populism, Racism, and White Supremacy in Rutherford County, North Carolina.* J. Timothy Cole. 2003
11. *The Brevard Rosenwald School: Black Education and Community Building in a Southern Appalachian Town, 1920–1966.* Betty J. Reed. 2004
12. *The Bristol Sessions: Writings About the Big Bang of Country Music.* Edited by Charles K. Wolfe and Ted Olson. 2005
13. *Community and Change in the North Carolina Mountains: Oral Histories and Profiles of People from Western Watauga County.* Compiled by Nannie Greene and Catherine Stokes Sheppard. 2006
14. *Ashe County: A History; A New Edition.* Arthur Lloyd Fletcher. 2009 [2006]
15. *The New River Controversy; A New Edition.* Thomas J. Schoenbaum. Epilogue by R. Seth Woodard. 2007
16. *The Blue Ridge Parkway by Foot: A Park Ranger's Memoir.* Tim Pegram. 2007
17. *James Still: Critical Essays on the Dean of Appalachian Literature.* Edited by Ted Olson and Kathy H. Olson. 2008
18. *Owsley County, Kentucky, and the Perpetuation of Poverty.* John R. Burch, Jr. 2008
19. *Asheville: A History.* Nan K. Chase. 2007
20. *Southern Appalachian Poetry: An Anthology of Works by 37 Poets.* Edited by Marita Garin. 2008
21. *Ball, Bat and Bitumen: A History of Coalfield Baseball in the Appalachian South.* L.M. Sutter. 2009
22. *The Frontier Nursing Service: America's First Rural Nurse-Midwife Service and School.* Marie Bartlett. 2009
23. *James Still in Interviews, Oral Histories and Memoirs.* Edited by Ted Olson. 2009
24. *The Millstone Quarries of Powell County, Kentucky.* Charles D. Hockensmith. 2009
25. *The Bibliography of Appalachia: More Than 4,700 Books, Articles, Monographs and Dissertations, Topically Arranged and Indexed.* Compiled by John R. Burch, Jr. 2009
26. *Appalachian Children's Literature: An Annotated Bibliography.* Compiled by Roberta Teague Herrin and Sheila Quinn Oliver. 2010
27. *Southern Appalachian Storytellers: Interviews with Sixteen Keepers of the Oral Tradition.* Edited by Saundra Gerrell Kelley. 2010
28. *Southern West Virginia and the Struggle for Modernity.* Christopher Dorsey. 2011

29. *George Scarbrough, Appalachian Poet: A Biographical and Literary Study with Unpublished Writings.* Randy Mackin. 2011

30. *The Water-Powered Mills of Floyd County, Virginia: Illustrated Histories, 1770–2010.* Franklin F. Webb and Ricky L. Cox. 2012

31. *School Segregation in Western North Carolina: A History, 1860s–1970s.* Betty Jamerson Reed. 2011

32. *The Ravenscroft School in Asheville: A History of the Institution and Its People and Buildings.* Dale Wayne Slusser. 2014

33. *The Ore Knob Mine Murders: The Crimes, the Investigation and the Trials.* Rose M. Haynes. 2013

34. *New Art of Willard Gayheart.* Willard Gayheart and Donia S. Eley. 2014

35. *Public Health in Appalachia: Essays from the Clinic and the Field.* Edited by Wendy Welch. 2014

36. *The Rhetoric of Appalachian Identity.* Todd Snyder. 2014

37. *African American and Cherokee Nurses in Appalachia: A History, 1900–1965.* Phoebe Ann Pollitt. 2016

38. *A Hospital for Ashe County: Four Generations of Appalachian Community Health Care.* Janet C. Pittard. 2016

39. *Dwight Diller: West Virginia Mountain Musician.* Lewis M. Stern. 2016

40. *The Brown Mountain Lights: History, Science and Human Nature Explain an Appalachian Mystery.* Wade Edward Speer. 2017

41. *Richard L. Davis and the Color Line in Ohio Coal: A Hocking Valley Mine Labor Organizer, 1862–1900.* Frans H. Doppen. 2016

42. *The Silent Appalachian: Wordless Mountaineers in Fiction, Film and Television.* Vicki Sigmon Collins. 2017

43. *The Trees of Ashe County, North Carolina.* Doug Munroe. 2017

44. *Melungeon Portraits: Exploring Kinship and Identity.* Tamara L. Stachowicz. 2018

45. *Always Been a Rambler: G.B. Grayson and Henry Whitter, Country Music Pioneers of Southern Appalachia.* Josh Beckworth. 2018

46. *Tommy Thompson: New-Timey String Band Musician.* Lewis M. Stern. 2019

47. *Appalachian Fiddler Albert Hash: The Last Leaf on the Tree.* Malcolm L. Smith with Edwin Lacy. 2020

Appalachian Fiddler Albert Hash
The Last Leaf on the Tree

MALCOLM L. SMITH
with EDWIN LACY

Foreword by WAYNE HENDERSON

CONTRIBUTIONS TO
SOUTHERN APPALACHIAN STUDIES, 47

McFarland & Company, Inc., Publishers
Jefferson, North Carolina

LIBRARY OF CONGRESS CATALOGUING-IN-PUBLICATION DATA

Names: Smith, Malcolm L., 1955– author. | Lacy, Edwin, 1959– author. | Henderson, Wayne, writer of foreword.
Title: Appalachian fiddler Albert Hash : the last leaf on the tree / Malcolm L. Smith with Edwin Lacy ; foreword by Wayne Henderson.
Description: Jefferson, North Carolina : McFarland & Company, Inc., Publishers, 2020 | Series: Contributions to southern Appalachian studies ; 47 | Includes bibliographical references and index.
Identifiers: LCCN 2020013887 | ISBN 9781476676425 (paperback : acid free paper) ∞
ISBN 9781476639406 (ebook)
Subjects: LCSH: Hash, Albert, 1917-1983. | Fiddlers—Virginia—Biography. | Luthiers—Virginia—Biogaphy.
Classification: LCC ML418.H35 S65 2020 | DDC 787.2092 [B]—dc23
LC record available at https://lccn.loc.gov/2020013887

BRITISH LIBRARY CATALOGUING DATA ARE AVAILABLE

ISBN (print) 978-1-4766-7642-5
ISBN (ebook) 978-1-4766-3940-6

© 2020 Malcolm L. Smith and Edwin Lacy. All rights reserved

No part of this book may be reproduced or transmitted in any form or by any means, electronic or mechanical, including photocopying or recording, or by any information storage and retrieval system, without permission in writing from the publisher.

Front cover: Albert Hash in his coat of many fiddles, 1973 (photograph by Martin Fox); *background* photograph of Mount Rogers, Virginia (Shutterstock/Rui Serra Maia)

Printed in the United States of America

McFarland & Company, Inc., Publishers
  Box 611, Jefferson, North Carolina 28640
    www.mcfarlandpub.com

To the memory of Thornton Spencer,
and to his wonderful family,
Emily, Kilby and Martha Spencer

Table of Contents

Foreword by Wayne Henderson — 1

Introduction by Malcolm L. Smith — 3

One—A Young Genius on Whitetop Mountain — 7
Two—An Appalachian Upbringing — 20
Three—Clocks, Machines and "Govn'ment Work" — 50
Four—Eric Clapton's Guitar — 72
Five—The Grooming of a Banjo Player — 89
Six—Bringing Whitetop to the World — 115
Seven—The Last Leaf on the Tree — 142
Eight—The Legacy of Albert Hash — 157

Appendix I: Discography: Albert Hash — 177
Appendix II: List of Known Recorded Tunes by Albert Hash (from Kilby Spencer) — 178
Chapter Notes — 181
Bibliography — 187
Index — 189

Foreword
by Wayne Henderson

It's about time someone wrote a book about Albert Hash. Any book about him is an important book. In my mind, Albert was an unusual person with unusual abilities. He was a folk hero. He was very important to the lives of many people here in the mountains.

Had I not met Albert Hash when I was 15, my life probably would have been very different. My dad, who was an old-time fiddler, used to take his fiddles to Albert for repair, so when he knew I had the hunger to build a guitar, that's where we went, to Albert's house in Lansing, North Carolina. When Albert brought out the parrot-headed fiddle he made with a gorgeous peacock carved in the back and put it in my hands and told me that he had made that fiddle, all with his own hands, it changed my life.

See, for many of us here in this area, Albert was the first real artist we'd ever met. We grew up like Albert, knowing that if we needed something we'd probably have to make it or fix it up ourselves. That's the mountain way of life. But Albert, he was the first to show me that what you made with your hands didn't just have to be useful, it could, at the same time, be beautiful. It could be art.

Albert not only encouraged me, he also fed my passion for building guitars. It wasn't just me, either. He encouraged and helped launch instrument builders and musicians across this area. My brother, Max, and I played in his band on the radio. He was someone I looked up to and wanted to be like. When I first met him, his artwork was more focused on clocks than fiddles. When I entered his house for the first time, I saw a beautiful grandfather clock. He had figured out every detail, every gear and wheel.

Like Albert, I had tried to make my first instrument as a young boy. I needed my own guitar, one that I had built to play in the mountain tra-

Foreword by Wayne Henderson

dition. Albert showed me the way to realize my dream. He shared ideas, wood and tools, and he praised me to no end when I brought him my first real guitar. He and his daughter, Audrey, did that for a lot of folks in this area and then taught a lot of them how to play their instruments, too.

I think Albert Hash was an important person. He was a self-made machinist, a self-made fiddle and clockmaker, a great fiddler and a fine gentleman to everyone who was lucky enough to know him. This is an important book about a great man. Read it.

Wayne Henderson's unique fingerpicking of old-time and bluegrass tunes has taken him to Carnegie Hall and his hand-built guitars are some of the most sought-after in the world. He was awarded a National Heritage Fellowship by the National Endowment for the Arts and has built guitars for Doc Watson, Eric Clapton and Peter Rowan. He was the subject of the book Clapton's Guitar: Watching Wayne Henderson Build the Perfect Instrument *in 2005. He has lived his entire life in Grayson County, Virginia.*

Introduction
by Malcolm L. Smith

Almost three years ago, on a beautiful Appalachian fall evening, I found myself sitting around a campfire in rural Floyd County, Virginia, with, as usual, my banjo, my left-hand fingers tickling the fretboard while my right hand drummed down across the head. At the end of a rousing version of "The Carroll County Breakdown," the minister at the gathering and one of my fellow musicians, Edwin Lacy, leaned in and asked me if he could talk to me. Right away, I worried that he might sense some noticeable spiritual crisis in me, or if I'd played the tune wrong.

What ensued was one of the greatest adventures in an adventure-filled life, the creation of the book you now hold in your hands. The journey from that moment to this one has led me into the lives and homes of some very extraordinary people, all of them not only gracious and encouraging, but also willing to dedicate themselves, their time, their energy and their resources to see this book come to fruition.

However, I should say that this project really started well before that moment around the campfire. It actually started when a kind and loving father, Casey Lacy, took his son, Edwin Lacy, to meet and play some music with a friend of his, someone teenage Edwin would become totally enamored with, like so many others had. Edwin, a young banjo prodigy from Wytheville, Virginia, was in his early teens. He would later make a professional career of old-time music and then, later still, reinvent himself as a Presbyterian minister and found the Wild Goose Uprising, a Christian gathering that utilizes rocking chairs instead of pews and creates a worshipping environment that emphasizes Appalachian traditions.

One Sunday, Edwin's father drove his son up the ever-winding, twisty Highway 58 in southern Grayson County to a small brick home on Cabin

Introduction by Malcolm L. Smith

Creek. There he met a remarkable Appalachian gentleman from Whitetop Mountain, Virginia, named Albert Hash.

That evening around the campfire Edwin told me with great passion about Albert and Edwin's dad taking him to Sunday afternoon gatherings at Albert's house. Although I had heard of Albert, I did not know much about him. I associated him with the Whitetop Mountain Band (whom I had heard of but was not very familiar with, as I did not own any of their recordings) and with one tune: "Hangman's Reel."

Subtly, and in that devious preacher sort of way, Edwin began coaxing me in. "I've got this project that you would be perfect for," he told me. Ordinarily, I would run away quickly if a minister said something like that to me. For some reason, this time I stayed put and listened. "I want you to help me write a biography of Albert Hash," he said.

Although I had been visiting the Blue Ridge and playing music in the summers for more than 40 years, I had only recently moved to the Appalachians. I spent most of my life in Kansas and New Hampshire, patiently waiting for the day I could finally escape the confines of higher education and just immerse myself in old-time music full time. I was no stranger to writing about old-time musicians, having written articles for years for *The Old-Time Herald* and *Sing Out!* magazines. I had also written lots of academic dribble.

The look in Edwin's eyes became fiery as he told me about Albert, how he had built his first fiddle as a young boy after dreaming how to do it, how he had helped the launch of Wayne Henderson's illustrious guitar-making career, and how he had touched the lives of countless other people. Edwin told me he had started this project in 2010 with the help of Albert's daughter, Audrey. He also told me about an interview he had conducted with Albert for a high school project and had converted to disc with increased fidelity. He also told me the whole project had lost momentum, and that after six years of procrastination, it was in danger of dying.

I told him I'd think about it. I should have known better. It seemed perfect. Spending my days studying among the highest peaks in Grayson County, meeting people who still reside in one of the most remote areas of the Appalachians, writing about the music and the people I love. I started out with a cardboard box full of scribbled notes, newspaper clippings, and a few photos that Audrey Hash had given Edwin. That and the interview Edwin had recorded.

Nearly three years later I am amazed at how much I've learned by

Introduction by Malcolm L. Smith

immersing myself, everyday, in the life of a true Appalachian gentleman, a musician, and an advocate for Appalachian culture.

I officially started this book by spending two amazing days in the remote guitar shop of a living legend, Wayne Henderson. Those two days Edwin and I spent most of our time rolling on the floor clutching our sides as Wayne told us story after hilarious story about his mentor and dear friend Albert Hash. During the second visit to Wayne, we were even let into his guitar vault to gawk at his incredible collection of instruments, including an Albert Hash fiddle, the only Albert Hash guitar in existence, and an Albert Hash mandolin.

That same day, we were invited to the home of Thornton and Emily Spencer in Haw Orchard, stopping at the nearby Haw Orchard Cemetery on the way to visit Albert's grave. In the Spencers' mountain home we listened intently as 82-year-old Thornton Spencer, smoking his cigarettes and drinking Dr Pepper, told us lovingly of his brother-in-law and his teaching Thornton how to fiddle, while Emily filled in details, dates and anecdotes. Suddenly, in the middle of this visit, Thornton stood up, his tall, lanky figure nearly touching the ceiling. He donned the black top hat that Albert had given him and grabbed his fiddle. We got a personal concert from one of America's national folk treasures right there in the living room. Now, a couple of years later, I have only great memories of Thornton, since he has passed on to join Albert and other Grayson County musicians in one hell of a great angel band.

Whenever we began to conduct one of the 100 hours of interviews that went into this book, Edwin and I would wink and nod, knowing we were going to hear two things, right at the beginning. It never failed. The interview would start something like this: "Oh, Albert, he was the nicest man I've ever met!" Next we would hear, "He was a genius in so many ways." We interviewed engineers, ministers, luthiers, musicians, folklorists, friends and families and we always heard the same two things.

We spent one winter's day cozy by the woodstove in fiddler Dean Sturgill's house, where he had grown up and never really left. We watched and were moved while Dean, nearly both deaf and blind, teared up while beautifully recounting a hike up Fees Ridge to hear his neighbor fiddle. On his way home the fireflies lit up a rain-filled sky and an entire forest. The memory of Albert, his music, the fireflies, the mountains, and Albert's spirit was still resonating in his mind some 60 years later.

We met professional musicians like John McCutcheon, Joe Thrift, and TV personality David Holt, who told of Albert's patience with them

Introduction by Malcolm L. Smith

as young musicians and of the encouragement and inspiration he gave them. We also met luthiers who have become masters of their craft who would have never built anything if it weren't for Albert's teachings, advice and unselfish sharing of plans, materials and tools.

All of these people taught us something not only about Albert, but also about Appalachian culture and Appalachian values. While many have become bitter in these mountains, usually because they feel they have been deprived of the middle-class dreams of big cars, fancy homes and money to burn, others, including most of the people we interviewed, have chosen to live the life that Albert modeled. One not driven by a quest for money, for "anxiety and alarm clocks," as Albert put it. They embraced the lifestyle and the economy of their mountain ancestors.

This incredible journey has taught me a lot about roots and branches and colorful leaves falling beautifully and gently to the ground to further the survival of the tree and, most important, to fertilize the new buds that will develop in the spring. I humbly ask that you read this book not just as a good story of a good man's life, but as a schematic, an instruction book and a diagram of a life well lived. Albert Hash, through his way of living and his way of playing, has given all a glimpse of what it truly means to be an "Appalachian hillbilly." Let us pray it is not a dying art form.

ONE

A Young Genius on Whitetop Mountain

Albert Hash woke to the soft and haunting song of the Hermit Thrush. The sun was just breaking over Phoenix Mountain and sparkling through the old-growth red spruce trees outside his bedroom window. He had been waiting for this day for what seemed like an eternity. He quickly woke two of his three brothers, Ernest and Rhudy, and begged them to get dressed in a hurry and to grab the guitar. They moved quickly and quietly through their three-room house, grabbing some of their mother's biscuits out of a tin. Together they quickly fed the woodstove and headed out to feed the chickens. Then, as they had done nearly every morning of their lives, they lined up outside the outhouse, the oldest, Rhudy, heading in first. Tingling with excitement, they breathed in the clean mountain air.

There was going to be a folk festival on top of the second highest peak in Virginia. For weeks the folks living near Whitetop Mountain in Grayson County had been buzzing with news of it. Fiddlers from as far away as Bristol and Jonesborough, Tennessee, West Virginia and Kentucky were coming to compete in the fiddle contest. It was rumored that singers, players and dancers from across the Blue Ridge were coming as well. Even Eleanor Roosevelt, First Lady of the United States, was going to be in attendance.[1]

For most of the spring and summer of 1933, 16-year-old Albert Hash had been busy carving, whittling and polishing a special fiddle to take to the event. Having built his first fiddle at age 10, young Albert had already become adept at whittling elaborate headstocks and necks, sizing and gluing the tops and bottoms to the carefully shaped sides of fiddle after fiddle. Working with wood had already become an important part of his life.

Who could have imagined that this poor, slightly gangly, and often sickly Appalachian teen would eventually build hundreds of fiddles in his lifetime? Who would reckon that this boy would one day help start the careers of countless luthiers, become a nationally renowned old-time fiddler, and teach many people how to fiddle? Who would have thought that the Virginia General Assembly would one day pause for several minutes to honor his life as he was laid to rest a few yards from his home near Whitetop Mountain, recognizing his having become a strong symbol of the best of Appalachian culture and life, a true Appalachian "mountain man"?

As morning brought light into the hollows of southwest Virginia on August 15, 1933, Albert carefully placed his latest and best fiddle in a flour sack. He did that to avoid the shame that some folks placed on playing of fiddle music and headed up the mountain in the Grayson Highlands from his home in Fees Branch.[2] As he and his brothers hiked higher and higher up the mountain, up into the clouds of August, beautiful, primitive, and powerful fiddle tunes echoed through Albert's mind.

They were pieces he had learned from listening carefully to his great uncle George Finley, his neighbor, Corbett Stamper, and traveling musicians like Grayson and Whitter. They were tunes played on rainy days, at family gatherings and at dances at the schoolhouse. They were tunes by Gid Tanner and the Skillet Lickers from Georgia and Fiddlin' Arthur Smith from Tennessee that he had heard on the Victrola their father had bought. Ancient tunes that had weathered their journeys from the old countries of Scotland and Ireland, from the early days of America, before the Civil War, tunes like "Johnson Boys," "Chicken Reel," "Cripple Creek," "Uncle Joe," and "Old Joe Clark" pulsated through him with a driving power all their own.

Albert was used to hiking his way through the mountains of Grayson County. In fact, most every morning he traipsed a little over four miles to get to Mt. Rogers High School. Many days he and his brothers had hauled cherry bark, ginseng, or corn nearly nine miles to the nearest store. The only real road in this part of the county was mostly a rough dirt wagon road with huge ruts worn in it, and on a wet day you would sink in the mud up to your knees, so he had learn to navigate the mountains by using the sun and reading the geography to follow the ridges and streams to his destination.

Whitetop Mountain had been chosen for this national celebration of mountain culture for a good reason. The Grayson Highlands region of Virginia and North Carolina where Albert lived was special. Because of its relative isolation, ballads and melodies that the first settlers of the region had brought with them, ancient tunes from across Europe and the bal-

One—A Young Genius on Whitetop Mountain

lads of Ireland and England as well as tunes from the indigenous Native Americans and the music brought by those of African heritage had become lodged in the hollows and backroads of the area and had become as much a part of the landscape as the rugged peaks themselves. The tunes were spread orally and seldom written down, and they and the dances that accompanied them had become a vital and beautiful part of mountain life.

The tunes and ballads of the region could be heard whenever the hard-working, dedicated and highly loyal residents needed to celebrate as a family or community: at weddings, funerals, town festivals and harvests, shuckings, stringings, dances and contests. They were also played and sung whenever the mountaineers needed to escape the burdens of their daily toil and worries, after the work was done or when the weather prevented work, or whenever they needed to pass on stories and traditions to their young, or whenever they shared the work of husking corn, canning food, stringing beans or building barns. These tunes, ballads and dances were part of the essential fabric of mountain life and had been so since the beginning of human life in the mountains.

Ballad collectors and folklorists who were prominent at the time such as Britain's Cecil Sharp, Pete and Mike Seeger's father and mother, Charles and Ruth, from Washington, D.C., the Warners from New York, and, later, Alan Lomax from the Smithsonian spent considerable time finding songs and ballads here. Later in Albert's life, he too would be a sought-after source of folklorists and tune collectors like Art Rosenbaum, Blanton Owen and Ray Alden.

The music of the mountains was pure like the water of the many springs that fed the creeks of the area. However, in 1933, just a few years after the "Big Bang" of country music in nearby Bristol at the famed recording sessions of 1927, the mountain streams of music had begun to be polluted. Many outsiders and city dwellers had begun to seek it and commercialize it. A new medium, radio, was still mysterious in the mountains, but stronger signals from Nashville and beyond began to find their way to receivers in the Appalachians.

The "Interstate Musical Festival on Whitetop Mountain" was one of several "folk festivals" that were sweeping the South. The festival creators and backers hoped to capitalize on the recent country and "hillbilly" music craze while at the same time showcasing local talent that was yet to be "discovered" by the record companies and the growing radio audience. It was also hoped by the promoters that when the attendees at these festivals heard this music in its native setting, these mountains, played by authentic musicians rather than mere imitators, they would continue to seek out the real thing and the audience would grow exponentially for old-time mountain music and dance.

This was the third festival on Whitetop, and over the course of the first two, the promoters had ironed out many of the logistical problems of holding a festival on top of one of the highest mountains in Virginia. They were expecting a crowd in the tens of thousands. Musicians, having heard of the prizes and the party that had accompanied the first two festivals, had been practicing fervently for the mountain dance, fiddle, banjo, dulcimer, harmonica, and string ensemble contests.

Nearly everyone looked forward to the evening's square dancing as well as the fabulous dinner that had been promised. It was even rumored that there might be an opportunity to meet the First Lady herself, Eleanor Roosevelt. A huge lodge had been constructed on the site, built in a rustic style using some of the huge spruce timbers that remained on Whitetop. The organizers had been working for a full year to make sure everything was ready.

Albert and his brothers' path up Whitetop was a well-worn one, but only recently. There may never had been a road there if it weren't for the timber companies that raided the area in the first years of the twentieth century, among them interests owned by the Roosevelts themselves. From before the states had been united, the remoteness of the Commonwealth of Virginia's highest peaks and the surrounding area had eluded those who tried to tame or even map them.

The earliest survey of the area was attempted by William Byrd in 1728. He had started somewhere in present-day Patrick County. His party gave up after nearly 241 miles of surveying because of "the abundance of rattlesnakes."[3] In 1749, a party led by two surveyors, Joshua Fry and Peter Jefferson, returned to the area and attempted to establish boundaries between Virginia and what was then called Carolina.

They marked a crooked line that was in dispute for many years, including a small notch of land that later created a strange notch in the boundaries. In the ensuing years, this area became the subject of many fights between Virginia, North Carolina and Tennessee. In fact, at one point this area was so in contention that moonshiners set up their stills within the area because no one was sure whose jurisdiction it was.

There is also a prevalent tale in southwest Virginia that the original survey line was influenced by the fact that the surveying party had heard of a local moonshine still in the area. As the story goes, the party took

One—A Young Genius on Whitetop Mountain

their heavy surveying chains with them in search of the still, and when they found it and its operator, they spent a wild night. In the morning, they took up the survey again from the still location, more than a mile and a half from their last survey line.[4]

Interestingly, the two men who created this survey would later become key figures in American legacies. Peter was the father of a son by the name of Thomas who would later become president, and Fry would become commander in chief during the French and Indian War, where he would be killed, leaving the position to his second in command, a young general named George Washington.

The Roosevelt family's investments in the area went back to the early 1800s. The circumstances that would lead to Eleanor Roosevelt's attendance at the 1933 festival, however, began when her father was exiled to the area. He had been among the liveliest members of the New York social set, known in the newspapers of the time as simply "the Swells." Crushed by the death of his industrialist father, Theodore Roosevelt, Sr., Elliott was a heavy drinker by the age of 20.[5]

In 1892, when his daughter who would later marry her cousin, also a Roosevelt, was just 10 years old, Elliott was sent to Abingdon, Virginia, to recuperate from alcoholism after attending a "treatment" center in Illinois. The fresh mountain air seemed to invigorate him, and he became active in building railroads, advising timber companies and meeting the locals in the area between Bristol and Whitetop. During this time, he wrote beautiful, loving letters to his daughter, despite his obvious depression, describing the people, the culture, and the music of the region. Eleanor would keep these letters the rest of her life.

Unfortunately, one of the things about the culture Elliott quickly discovered was the local apple brandy, a specialty of the local moonshiners. Back in New York, Eleanor's mother fell ill, and for some time Elliott was asked by the family not to travel back to see her, increasing his depression and his drinking. When he finally did go to her funeral, he was convinced to relinquish custody of his daughter and son and was suddenly without family. In 1893, tragedy came again when his three-year-old son died of scarlet fever.

Although he continued to write his daughter advice and depictions of life in southwest Virginia, his depression and his alcoholism worsened. In 1894, his tumultuous life came to an end in New York City, with heart failure and complications of alcoholism the official cause of death, but suicidal behavior including climbing out of a window onto a roof among the unofficial reasons. His daughter saw that his love for the mountains of Virginia and her people had been one of the bright spots in his troubled life and saw the 1933 Whitetop festival as a way to be closer to her father's memory.

As Albert and his brothers climbed higher up the road to Whitetop's summit, they took in the air sweetened by the smell of the Appalachian red spruce that formed the "black cap" on the summit of the mountain. This tree was just beginning to become important in Albert's life. Already he had learned of its incredible qualities that made it perfect as a tone wood. Its strength in spite of its lightness in weight was complemented by its ability to transmit tones with richness and velocity. It provided high volume as a fiddle top and rang with complex overtones.

As Albert reached the top of Whitetop Mountain, he could hardly believe what he saw. There were more than 12,000 folks on the rounded peak, roaming through exhibits, parking cars and corralling horses, or lining up outside a huge circus tent to listen to or play in the contests. This was far more people than Albert had ever seen gathered in one place, let alone on top of his beloved Whitetop. There were dignitaries from across the world, there to see and hear the music and dancing of the Blue Ridge Mountains. They were there to hear Albert's music, his by right and heritage.

He had never seen so many people nor heard such a roar of excitement in his life. The hair on the back of Albert's neck stood up as he clutched the flour sack around his fiddle and watched string bands like the Dixie Serenaders from East Radford, Virginia, the Moonlight Ramblers from Lansing, North Carolina, and the Whitetop Jiggers from Bristol. There was Jack Reedy with his banjo, playing "Jenny Put the Kettle On" to a huge crowd, with Frank Blevins, one of Albert's favorites, on fiddle. And there was the First Lady herself, posing for autographs on the steps of the pavilion.

The air around him smelled of the barbeque pork being prepared and served by local ladies from Konnarock. Albert listened and even tried to play along as fiddlers, banjo players, guitar players and singers took the stage. Then the clog dancing competition began, and Albert was asked to join the band on stage! He ran to the stage, threw off the flour sack around his fiddle and cut loose on his version of "Arkansas Traveler."

After a few tunes, as he came down off the stage for some barbeque, a man he thought he recognized approached him. He was sharply dressed in a black suit and a black tie, and he was carrying a guitar and a harmon-

One—A Young Genius on Whitetop Mountain

ica. When he introduced himself as Henry Whitter, a Fries, Virginia, millworker turned musician, Albert nearly dropped his fiddle in astonishment. He didn't know what to say.

Whitter had often been in the papers and on countless promotional bulletins that Albert had seen around the mountains. Mr. Whitter had, until a tragedy in 1930 took the life of his partner, been part of the most popular mountain duo in the country, Grayson and Whitter. Henry had only met blind musician J.B. Grayson three years before, but they had quickly established themselves at the top of the emerging country or hillbilly music market.

Mr. Whitter had recently been recorded as part of the legendary "Bris-

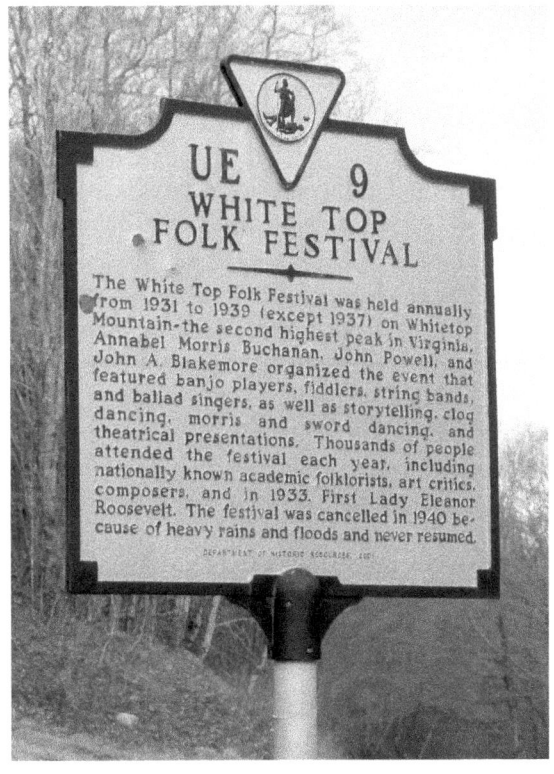

Sign commemorating the Whitetop Mountain music festivals of the 1930s on Whitetop Mountain Road (photograph by Jim Kacsmarik).

tol Sessions." The recordings were becoming all the rage in places like New York City and Nashville. Whitter himself had been recording since 1923 and had a long-established reputation as a mountain minstrel, recording "The Wreck of the Old Southern 97," "Lonesome Road Blues," and "New River Train," songs that were to become standards in mountain related music.[6]

As Albert stood staring at Mr. Whitter, he couldn't quite come up with words to speak. He had spent hours and hours listening to Grayson and Whitter records on the small gramophone his dad had bought. He had tried to learn every fiddle riff that Grayson had played. Mr. Whitter smiled and quietly asked him if he might be available to play a few songs with him. So off the two went, into the shade of the Adirondack spruce in the high elevation of Whitetop and played and sang together. Their fiddle and guitar created a sound that carried down to the crowds below, and some attendees climbed the hill to join them.

As Henry and Albert paused for a moment, a very prestigious-looking gentleman approached them and introduced himself as Colonel Kettle from England. As he shook Albert's hand, he asked if he might hold Albert's fiddle. As he held it delicately, looking at the hand-carved bird on the head and the elaborate carvings on the back, he asked Albert if he might take a picture of it.

It was at that exact moment, Albert would recall nearly 50 years later, that he realized he didn't need to hide his fiddles or his fiddling any longer. "I realized it was just more serious than I had heard the music was." He would say, "I felt justified in what I was doing." During the next few years, Albert would end up accompanying Henry Whitter at performances throughout the mountains and begin a five-decade career as a mountain musician and carver of fine spruce fiddles. Nearly a hundred years after his birth, his fiddles would be highly sought after, coveted, and on display in places like the Smithsonian, the Blue Ridge Music Center, and museums throughout the South.[7]

Glue, Horsehair, a Packing Crate and Sewing Pins

The journey that would take Albert to the folk festival on top of Whitetop Mountain had really begun five years earlier when Albert was about nine years old. Living high in the mountains, in poverty, Albert had developed, at a very young age, a great passion for the fiddle. Sometimes he would hear George Finley play at schoolhouse dances, rollicking back and forth on his chair as his fiddle bow danced. Albert never forgot the reverence that his great uncle George felt for that prized instrument. It hung in a special place where no one was allowed to touch it, and he would only play it if greatly coaxed and begged.

He quickly learned how Uncle George's aged hands had to be in the right mood to play. He watched carefully how he carefully tucked his fiddle into the top of his vest to hold it in place. He had an unusually large white mustache that came within an inch of his bow as he played. Once Albert witnessed his Uncle George rocking so hard in his chair while playing that he rocked himself right off the schoolhouse stage, yelling, "Take care of my fiddle!" as he hit the floor on his back![8]

One—A Young Genius on Whitetop Mountain

The very first time he heard the fiddle, though, his brothers said he went running and screaming down the road away from the sound. He had covered his ears, afraid of what the sound might do to him. No one really thought Albert would ever want to play the fiddle.

Albert's parents, Abraham Hash and Della Long, were subsistence farmers, or at least Della was, trying to eke out food and a living from the hilly, stony red-clay soil of Fees Branch. Albert and his three brothers, Rhudy, Dennis and Ernest, learned to appreciate music and dance at an early age as their mother sang the old ballads of the mountains to them in their cribs. Their mother's brother, Emmet Long, was an accomplished clawhammer style banjo player who had been taught by his uncle who was also named Emmet Long. The second Emmet would eventually teach Jont Blevins, an influential area musician in Albert's life, to play banjo.[9]

While learning the hard lessons of farming in Appalachia, Albert and his brothers also learned the importance of music in the rhythm of Appalachian life. Two of his brothers wanted to play guitar. His oldest brother, Rhudy, later became a great dancer who would dance with the Ringling Bros. Circus. But it was Albert who developed a special passion for the ancient music of the mountains.

Albert never forgot the exact moment he fell totally in love with the fiddle. He and his mother had gotten up early to hoe a cornfield that they rented from a neighbor, Corbett Stamper, high in the mountains. After two hours or so of backbreaking work, a mountain downpour began and sent them fleeing to the shelter of Corbett's porch. After the thunder and lightning had passed Corbett went inside and pulled his fiddle from under the bed and brought it out to the porch. He sat close to Albert and his mother and began to play "Sally Goodin" and "Old Joe Clark."

Eight-year-old Albert was between his mother's knees, swaying to the tunes that seemed to be dancing out of the sound holes in the fiddle. He watched the mesmerizing flow of the fiddle bow until Corbett rested between songs. Albert leaned close to his mother and whispered in her ear. She grinned when she heard the boy's shy but earnest request. "Corbett, Albert wants you to play some more tunes," his mother said, and the morning flew by as Albert's mind and heart were filled with the music of the mountains.[10]

That was it. Those tunes were with Albert from that morning on. He would hum them as he worked, or as he walked the three miles to the nearest store to buy supplies for his parents. He memorized the highs and lows of every melody and even the look of contentment Corbett had on his face as he played. And he would stare longingly at the three-dollar fiddle in the general store. He had to have a fiddle. That was all there was to it.

He begged his parents for one, but there was no money. If buying one was impossible, maybe he could figure out how to make one. Appalachian people had a genius for making the things they couldn't afford to buy, often ending up with better versions than the store-bought models.

So he began to study Uncle George's fiddle hanging on the wall every chance he got, memorizing the curves of the sound holes and the shape of the neck, top, and sides. He would study how the strings attached, and how the bridge that held those strings was shaped. He pondered and worried over it day and night.

Then one night in 1927, Albert, at the age of nine, dreamed about making a fiddle. In his dream he saw himself carving the top and back and sides. He saw the neck taking shape as he whittled away every bit of wood that wasn't a neck. He saw himself stretching the hair of the bow and playing those wonderful tunes on his very own fiddle. He carefully worked out every aspect of building his first fiddle. In his dream the fiddle not only played, it played beautiful music just like Uncle George and Corbett Stamper played.

Albert loved to tell the story of rising the next morning and stealing away quickly to the barn. There, checking to make sure that no one was watching him use the family tools, he drew the outline of a fiddle on the sides of a pine packing crate and cut out a top and back using the family's only precious hand saw. He found some other thick wood to carve into sides, shaping the curves with a chisel fashioned from a large nail and a piece of railroad track for a hammer. He called the sides "rims." Out of a scrap of walnut, he carved the scroll of the neck and pinned the neck to the body. Albert took a wood burning tool and carefully burnt holes into the neck he had carved, under the scroll he had fashioned. Then he carefully whittled pegs to fit into those holes to hold the strings and adjust them when needed. His dream was beginning to come true!

Albert then carefully snuck into the house and pulled several sewing pins from his mother's pincushion. Since there was no glue to be had, he carefully nailed and tacked the top and the back of the fiddle to the sides using those pins. Next to the barn, he found an old rusted screen door. He painstakingly pulled pieces of screen wire from it and tacked them across the fiddle. He could pluck those wires and get a sound, but it didn't yet make music like a fiddle.

A couple of days later, Albert was sitting near a fence where a neigh-

One—A Young Genius on Whitetop Mountain

bor was plowing a field. The neighbor leaned over the fence and got Albert's attention. "Boy," he said, "if you'll go over to the Flattop store and get me a can of Prince Albert tobacco, I'll give you a quarter." Albert couldn't believe his good fortune. He nearly ran the three miles to the store to get the can of tobacco. When he got there, just as he suspected, sitting in the display case was a brand-new set of fiddle strings priced at 25 cents. He brought a set back and replaced the screen wire with real strings.

Then he sat, holding his fiddle for a couple of days, contemplating how to make a fiddle bow. One morning he set out for a nearby wetlands area and brought back a nice elder stick, about the right size. The elder was hollow; it was easy to fashion into the shape of a bow. Now all Albert needed was bow hair to string it with. He knew from listening to his great uncle talk that bows were made of horsehair. Having noticed that every bow he'd seen was white, Albert figured he would have to find a white-tailed horse to provide him bow hair.

He walked hills and hollers in the area looking for a white-tailed horse. Finally, it dawned on him that the mailman, who came to their farm nearly every day, had a white-tailed steed. So 10-year-old Albert set about a surveillance operation on the horse. He discovered that every day at noon, the mailman would corral his horse at a neighbor's farm while he sat down to eat his lunch in the nearby barn.

Albert brought along his brother Dennis for support, headed to the farm, and the two boys chased the horse into a corner of the fence. Then Albert ran to the outside of the fence while Dennis kept the horse cornered. Albert reached through the fence and grabbed the horse's tail with both hands, as tight as he possibly could. Then both boys let out a yell and the horse took off as fast as he could. Albert held on with all his might as the horse almost pulled him through the fence. And then, with a great leap, the horse was gone! Albert looked down and found long white hairs in each of his hands.

He ran all the way home to find his homemade elder bow. He tied the white horsehair around each end of the stick and beamed as he held his homemade bow. He ran to the barn and grabbed his fiddle and sat down on a firewood chopping block to play his very first tune on the fiddle he had worked so hard to create. This was the moment he had dreamed of for so long. But as he fingered the walnut neck and ran the bow across the strings, nothing came out. Albert was crushed. He sat there on that chopping block with his heart breaking. What had he done wrong?

About that time an older neighbor boy came walking by and saw Albert sitting there scratching the bow across the strings to no avail. The boy could play a few tunes on a fiddle. He told Albert, "I know what's wrong. You've got to have some resin on that bow to get a sound." He said, "I'm goin' up yonder to play a dance, but I'll be back later and bring you some resin." And that's what he did. He came back later that evening, while Albert was still sitting on the chopping block, waiting patiently. He

A teenage Albert Hash posing with a banjo. Although Albert built a few banjos in his lifetime, he rarely, if ever, actually played one (courtesy Carla Osborne).

One—A Young Genius on Whitetop Mountain

took the fiddle from Albert, carefully rosined up the bow, then laid in the woodchips with his head on the chopping-block, looking at the stars, and played a tune. Then he played another one. Albert thought he might cry. Music from his own fiddle!

When the neighbor played all he was going to play, he handed the fiddle back to Albert and went on his way. Albert took the fiddle and ran to what would become his favorite place to play, a little warm space behind the wood cookstove where he wouldn't bother anybody and tried to play the tunes that the neighbor had just played. As he did, all the household cats that had been warming their backs against the stove shrieked and ran away.[11]

Regardless of what the cats thought, Albert's first fiddle made music that was beautiful to his ears. But not as beautiful as the hundreds and hundreds of other fiddles he would carefully and painstakingly carve throughout his lifetime and not nearly as sweet as the hundreds and hundreds of tunes that would be played on them. The first tune that fiddle sang out was an old gospel song his mother knew, "Way Over in the Promised Land." As Albert rocked his homemade and well-rosined bow across the strings of his very own fiddle and heard the notes of a mountain melody sing out from it, he felt content.

Ironically, Albert's first fiddle's life was short lived. Although it would have been a great museum piece at the Smithsonian, the reality is that a few months after he painstakingly built it, one of his brothers accidently sat on it and smashed it into small pieces.

Two

An Appalachian Upbringing

A Mountain of Music

Grayson County encompasses much of the southwest of the Commonwealth of Virginia. It also holds much of its beauty. Beginning high on the Blue Ridge plateau in Galax, it rises to encompass the two highest peaks in the state, Whitetop Mountain and Mt. Rogers. Wild ponies roam the beautiful Grayson Highlands Park that covers a vast area of the county. The ponies that delight visitors on the Appalachian Trail were brought from islands on the outer banks of North Carolina in the early part of the century to control brush at high elevations.

The oldest river in the United States, the fabled New River of song and story, flows through much of the county, carrying the music of the mountains from south to north. From its settlement in the early 1700s, the county has had traditional music tilled into its soil, from Cherokee chants to mountain ballads and African songs to ancient fiddle tunes that came from Scotland, Ireland, England, France and Germany. And each of those traditions has attracted various types of dances, from those done around campfires to those performed on wooden floors.

On June 17, 1917, just as the wildflowers and the mountain laurel began to bloom, Albert Lillard Hash was born into the home of Abraham Lincoln Hash and Della Mae Long near Rugby, Virginia, in the Grayson County highlands. In the early 1900s the area was bustling with activity. Timber interests from New York, Pennsylvania, and points north, including one owned by Eleanor Roosevelt's father, had deeply invested in the region's old growth timber including acres and acres of Appalachian red spruce. Thousands and thousands of these majestic trees were being clear cut and dragged by horse and wagon to Konnarock and Whitetop where

Two—An Appalachian Upbringing

the Virginia Creeper, a steep railroad run with steam engines, had been built to haul the timber down to sawmills in Damascus, Abingdon and beyond.[1]

The lives of the residents of this area in the early 1900s still, in many ways, resembled the lives of their immigrant forefathers who settled here. The small mountain cabins and shacks of the area did not have electricity until the late 1950s and early '60s. According to the county census, as late as 1940, more than 95 percent of the homes in Grayson County lacked a bathtub or shower, 99 percent lacked central heat, and only 1 percent cooked with electricity, gas, gasoline or kerosene. Less than 30 percent of these homes had an automobile of any kind.[2] Albert's family, living high on Fees Ridge, had none of the modern conveniences, and for all practical purposes they carried on life in the mountains much as it had been lived since the first settlers had come from the North.

Once the timber barons left, folks had to make do with what they had. Jobs were scarce and most families just tried to subsist by gathering what they could of mountain herbs and scratching out corn and livestock feed in the rocky soil. Most of the timber companies that clear cut much of the native trees had brought their own lumberjacks from northern camps and locals were left to do menial tasks for the invading armies with axes and crosscut saws.

By the 1920s, when Albert built his first fiddle, most of the timber had been harvested and the locals were left digging stumps and granite out of the remaining fields to try to dig furrows for vegetable seeds and mountain herbs. Although the high mountain summers were cool and wet, the winters were often harsh, and families had to labor long hours just to manage their woodlots to keep warm. Thankfully, the timber companies had left many remnants to burn.

When asked about how he grew up, Albert put it this way: "We was isolated and we depended on each other for the things that we needed and we depended on ourselves for things that we needed." This self-reliance and appreciation of family were ingrained in Albert and his neighbors from their earliest years. If he needed a fiddle, he would have to build it. If his little brother needed a toy, he would have to carve it. If he needed new clothes, he would have to share his brothers.[3]

This isolation was both geographic and a result of the attitude surrounding the proud mountain heritage and culture in which Albert was raised. In describing the early 1900s in Grayson County, author Sherree Tannen observed:

The townspeople and citizens of numerous villages assimilated into the mainstream of what would prove to be a perceptible American Culture. Yet, the mountaineer withdrew from the world into a remote universe distinctly his own. His customs, beliefs and values were well defined by the beginning of the twentieth century. Thus, one hundred years after the settling of the mountains the men, women and children of White Top Mountain, Brushy Mountain and Iron Mountain continued to live much as their pioneer ancestors had done. The farther they retreated to the mountains, the more their lives were dominated by poverty and resistance to the changing culture.[4]

Albert's father, Abraham Lincoln Hash, had been a schoolteacher in the area when he met and started a family with Della Mae Long. The fact

Abraham Lincoln Hash, Albert's father, ca. 1920 (courtesy Rebecca Hash Gilbert).

Two—An Appalachian Upbringing

that he had been named after the Union president upon his birth in 1886 says a lot about the Hash family and their neighbors' feelings about the Civil War. Though Grayson County did have one regiment in the Confederacy based in Elk Creek, most of the residents were apathetic, at best, about fighting for wealthy people's right to own slaves. The settlers who came to this region were fiercely independent, yet fiercely loyal to their neighbors. That was the way with Albert's family.

Albert's parents never married, partly due to his father's job with the railroad and, possibly, his reluctance to commit. It may also have had a lot to do with the fact that Della Mae was a very independent and self-reliant woman, at least in her younger years. She took on the raising of three boys on her own in much the same way she took on corn hoeing and crop gathering: fiercely determined.

Abraham Hash never played an instrument; he had lost a hand in the service, some say it was during World War I, others say it was due to a hunting accident. The music that Albert heard in his early years came mostly from his mother, who knew many of the old mountain ballads; from his neighbor, Corbett Stamper, and his fiddling great uncle, George Finley; and later from a Victrola that his father brought home. On the early record player he carefully listened to the music of Grayson and Whitter, Gid Tanner and the Skillet Lickers, and Fiddlin' Arthur Smith, among others, and later he would learn their fiddle licks note for note on his homemade fiddles.

As his fiddle prowess became known, as a teenager, Albert began to discover the variety of musicians who lived in the county and his repertoire began to grow exponentially, as he walked from farm to farm, learning the repertoires of the older fiddlers of Grayson County. This would sometimes require hours of walking over trails and old wagon roads just to learn a new song or two.

The isolation of the area of Grayson County where Albert's family lived made it difficult to realize the incredible diversity of music that surrounded him during his early years. His neighbor, Corbett Stamper, was a fiddler of some reputation as was his great uncle, George Finley, who Albert occasionally heard when he was small and whose repertoire he would learn when he was in high school. In Rugby, just a few miles away, was Walter Henderson (father to guitar builder Wayne Henderson), a fine old-time fiddler and string band performer. Close by was guitarist E.C. (Estil Cortez) Ball and his wife Orna who were recording artists. All of this mountain music would prove integral to Albert's later life.

This music, the mountain music of Grayson County, was a part of the very fabric of the area. It was present at bean stringings and barn buildings, at weddings and funerals, during schoolhouse dances and church dinners and at community celebrations of everything from the ripening of ramps in the spring to shucking corn in the summer. Born in the mountains, grown in the mountains, this music was largely hidden away in the hollers and on the steep hillsides from much of the general population until the advent of festivals and field recordings. It was truly music that grew out of and celebrated the simple, hard, yet joyful life of the Blue Ridge mountaineer.

The region, in general, was teeming with old-time country musicians who made names for themselves as the new age of hillbilly music dawned. Henry Whitter (who Albert later toured with) from Fries, Virginia, was featured on the highly touted Bristol recordings. On the backside of Whitetop near Bristol was the famous Carter Fold, the family home of A.P. and Mother Maybelle Carter, who became radio pioneers following the "Big Bang" in Bristol. The 1927 Bristol recording sessions and the highly attended Whitetop Mountain folk festivals in the 1930s brought many other local Virginia musicians to prominence from all sides of the mountain including the Stoneman Family, "Uncle" Norman Edmonds, the Shelor/Blackford family, Eck Dunford and many more.

Northward, in Galax, were such greats as banjoist Wade Ward, fiddler Ernest Stoneman, and a host of others including John Rector and his band, the Hill Billies. In close proximity to Galax, Mt. Airy, North Carolina, was producing great musicians like Ben Jarrell, father to the legendary Tommy Jarrell who would, like Albert, inspire a generation to take up and play old-time music in the 1960s and '70s.

The music of the Blue Ridge and particularly that of Grayson County, Virginia, was a unique blend of cultural influences. In its tones could be heard music from Africa brought by slaves, music of relocated Cherokee tribe members, the sea songs of those who set sail from Europe, the music of Ireland, Great Britain, Germany, all with the unique stamp of Appalachian settlers who played and danced to this music as a regular part of their mountain lives.

They played and danced for fun, for relaxation, and to commence communal work as well as to escape and offset the burdens of their extremely hard and self-reliant existences. The music got trapped down in the hollers and on the mountaintops of the Blue Ridge, where it ripened and gained both a structure and an essence of its own, from sweet waltzes

Two—An Appalachian Upbringing

to crazy fast dance numbers with ancient ballads sprinkled in between. It was into this vibrant musical culture that Albert was born.[5]

When Albert first started to deeply yearn to play music on instruments he knew he could build, the guitar was not commonplace. The songs of the mountains were usually played on fiddles and banjos, with the occasional but rare piano or pump organ chiming in. The banjo, it seemed, was somewhat easier to build than the fiddle, so many homes had a mountain-made banjo on the wall often complete with a groundhog-hide head. In the early part of the century, mass-producing wizardry from Sears and Roebuck and large conglomerates like Montgomery Ward made fiddles readily available to a rural public, either through mail order or through purchase at nearly every small country store.

The combination of fiddle and banjo duets was and still is at the root of the upper Grayson sound, even as the guitar and, later, the upright bass assimilated into the mountain sound. Fiddle and banjo duets required a strong rhythmic approach on the banjo, creating the "bass end" and chord structure to keep the beat, but they also required the banjoist to help keep the melody alive, accentuating the notes of the fiddle. This give and take of banjo and fiddle is still alive in the music near Whitetop today, much to the credit of Albert and his family, friends and neighbors.

Rural dry goods shops often stocked not only fiddles but also cases, strings and rosin. However, to many rural Depression-era families like Albert's, who were trying to subsist on small farms, the instruments' $6- to $10-price tags made them accessible to the mountaineers only in dreams. As the success of the Hawaiian-born guitar spread across the country, local stores and the big "wish book" stores began to carry them and make them more accessible and affordable to Appalachians. As Albert entered high school, some of his classmates were already playing guitars and his brothers quickly caught on to the new instrument.

It was little wonder that a team of national folklorists and enthusiasts embraced Whitetop Mountain to stage a regional and national celebration of Appalachian culture and music in the early 1930s. By then, the region was literally teeming with great musicians, many of whom had learned to play on home-built banjos and cigar-box fiddles. The festivals featured local fiddlers, string bands, ballad singers and dancers who practiced clogging and flatfooting, especially the local "buck and wing." It offered prizes for fiddlers, singers, banjoists, bands and dancers. It also brought some much-needed economic relief to a struggling area.

Ironically, the blue ribbon winner at the 1933 Whitetop festival for old-time dance was "Uncle" Bud Spencer, who was a grandfather to Albert's future wife, Ethel, as well as to arguably Albert's best student and fiddling partner, Thornton Spencer. Uncle Bud's blue ribbon was ceremoniously pinned to his chest by none other than Mrs. Roosevelt herself. The story of his dancing for the First Lady became legendary in the county.[6]

It was, for mountain musicians like Albert, a revelation that the home-grown and home-sewn music of the Blue Ridge appealed to a wider national audience, even to the wife of President Roosevelt. During the last year of the Whitetop festival, 1935, another event was formed that would forever transform local Grayson County music to a national and international phenomenon: the first Galax Old Fiddlers Convention was convened at the town park. It would quickly overtake and overshadow the Whitetop Festival as *the* festival of mountain culture. This

Uncle Bud Spencer, Thornton and Ethel Spencer's grandfather, at the 1933 Whitetop Mountain Festival, where he was awarded a first place ribbon by Eleanor Roosevelt. The musicians are unidentified (courtesy Mark Sanderford).

annual contest and showplace for old-time and bluegrass music quickly evolved into one of the most important mountain music events in the world. It brought international recognition to the musicians of Grayson County and continues to do so to this day, emphasizing both bluegrass and old-time music.

Started by the Galax Moose Lodge, the festival, from its inception, was meant "to keep alive the memories and sentiments of days gone by and make it possible for people of today to hear and enjoy the tunes of yesterday." Like the Whitetop festival, the Galax festival started by featuring mainly local fiddlers like Emmett Lundy and Eck Dunford and featured local bands like the Bogtrotters and the Carroll County Ramblers but quickly grew to attract both regional and national musicians in the competitions and in the audience. Albert would attend and perform at the festival many times over the years and take home several ribbons.

A Self-Reliant Family

Albert had three brothers: Rhudy Lee, born in 1911; Dennis, born in 1913; and Ernest, born in 1922. Rhudy and Ernest were both musicians and could play a variety of instruments and often backed Albert up on guitar and banjo in his earliest performances. Dennis, who could play the banjo, became a dancer of some renown and tap-danced for a couple of years with the Ringling Bros. Circus, seeing the country by rail. All three brothers met and married three sisters from nearby Jefferson, North Carolina, and all three left the area in the early 1940s seeking factory work elsewhere.

While Albert, Ernest, and Rhudy headed toward the wartime plants near the naval yard in the U.S. capital, Dennis took a different path. He headed out to see some of the country. He danced when he could, rode rails sometimes, and was a traveller or hobo for a few years, following the life described by Woody Guthrie's Depression-era songs.

Ernest and Dennis and their families joined Albert during the war years working at a submarine plant in northern Virginia as sort of an alternative to service. Eventually, after spending some time in New Jersey, all three brothers settled in the more northern regions of Virginia, making many trips back to Grayson County to visit Albert and his family. They always considered Albert's house in the mountains their home, and they and their children have many fond memories of climbing mountains and

Appalachian Fiddler Albert Hash

Albert Hash and his brothers, August 1956. From left, Dennis, Albert, Ernest and Rhudy Hash (courtesy Kilby Spencer).

hiking with Albert, watching him work in his woodshop, and the music parties that seemed to be always happening at his house.[7]

Albert was smaller and much frailer than his brothers and as a child often stayed home and tended to housework while his brothers and mother hoed the family corn plot and spent hours harvesting bark and herbs to sell at local stores as ingredients in teas, tinctures and medicines. For a while, one of the primary crops of the area was catnip, while cherry bark, mint and even ginseng were harvested in quantity and sold at local stores.

Chestnuts were also plentiful. Although mostly gone from the mountains now, due to generations of blight, chestnuts and their smaller relatives, chinquapin nuts, provided valuable commodities for mountain folks to sell. The nuts were both plentiful and delicious and added to the number of natural resources that Albert and his family could sell.

"Well, you did anything you could to pick up an extra dollar," Albert told one interviewer. "You could raise a little bit of stuff on the farm, but not enough to say anything. Maybe someone would want a little bit of work done on an old house—I've done carpentry work, I've done everything," he said.[8]

Two—An Appalachian Upbringing

Abraham Lincoln Hash, by all accounts, was not much of a family man. After teaching, he became a bookkeeper with the Virginia Supply railroad company and spent much of his time working on and living in a boxcar. His trips home were sporadic and he contributed very little to the work his boys and their mother were doing on their farm. The family only saw him once in a while. The family lived in remote Fees Gap, and for most of Albert's early life they had no means of transportation other than a horse. They rented a small cornfield from the family of their neighbor Corbett Stamper, who first introduced Albert to fiddling, and Della Mae and the boys toiled to plant and harvest small corn crops on their own.

Albert described his early years this way:

> It was the years of the Depression in this country, times was so tough that there wasn't a dime for anything. The timber had just been cut out and there was no timber to work in any more. It's not a farming country through here, you know, so you just had to get in the woods and dig roots and gather herbs and so on and dry them to sell to get yourself something to eat. So, if a fiddle had've costed a dime I couldn't have afforded one, nor my folks could have. It took everything we had to live on.[9]

Albert did not attend school until he was 10. The nearest school was just too far from his home to walk, and he was often needed at home to help with the chores and to care for his little brother. Finally, at 10, he stayed with his grandpa, closer to Wolf Knob School. He had a strong motivator to go to school. If he would go every day and stay in school so he could attend Mt. Rogers High School, his father promised him a store-bought fiddle. Albert kept his part of the bargain. He assumed a store-bought fiddle would play better and easier than the one he had built.

Once Albert got the fiddle, he immediately disassembled it to see how it was put together. He studied the bracing and sound post and the thicknesses of the top, back and sides. His second, third, and fourth fiddles were built using the exact dimensions of that store-bought instrument. Later, he ordered some fiddle plans through the mail and altered his design. Although it was precious to him because he had earned it, Albert never played that store-bought fiddle much. He just felt that the fiddles he made sounded and played much better, but he kept that fiddle all of his life, hanging on the wall of his shop, to remind him of an absent father's love.

Abraham died in 1936, when Albert was 19. On the day of his father's death, Albert had just finished a fiddle in his honor and was on the way to show it to him when he met a neighbor who told him his father had died.

Heartbroken, Albert felt abandoned by his father once again.[10] Albert's mother, Della May, later was married to Thomas Reedy, a local man who fiddled some, and lived with him until his death in 1959. Albert credited Tom Reedy for teaching him many fiddle tunes and he always had nice things to say about Tom, but for the most part the strength of their relationship is unknown.

Playin' Out

Shortly after starting school at the age of 10, Albert began to make school friends who also played music. Albert would regale his new friends with the tunes he had learned on the Victrola and ones he had heard Corbett Stamper or his great uncle George Finley play. One of the boys at school, Bruce Duvall, owned one of the first guitars in the area and Albert liked the way that Bruce backed up his fiddling. Bruce and Albert caught the attention of a local minister and were asked to play for a community event at his church. It would be Albert's first time playing anywhere except behind the woodstove or on the front porch. Years later, he recounted his first public performance to interviewer Frank Weston:

> We had a little redheaded preacher lived down the creek down here, very fine preacher. They would have these plays at the ending of the school term and parents would come in, some of them thought that they were smart enough to make speeches.

Della Mae Long Reedy, Albert's mother, ca. 1962. She lived with Abraham Lincoln Hash and later married Tom Reedy (courtesy Carla Osborne).

Two—An Appalachian Upbringing

> Me and my little friend Bruce Duvall were musicians for the play, he could play the guitar well, and I played the fiddle.
>
> They had us back behind of a little curtain; Ms. Alta Perkins, our teacher, told us that after each act of the play or speech, we would play a tune. Well, we were getting along pretty well. Then, it was time that Preacher Murphy gave a speech and then led a prayer. We figured we better have a good 'un picked out for him. So, as soon as he stopped, we lit into playing Old Molly Hare as fast as we could. Here Ms. Alta came running, saying, "Not now, boys, not this time!" And that was the first show I played out.[11]

After that first concert, Albert would spend almost 60 years playing in schools, fire stations, town halls and concert halls, festivals, contests and radio stations across the region. His fiddling would take him from the mountains of Grayson to the hallowed halls of the Smithsonian Institution in Washington, D.C., the concert halls of the Berkshires and college campuses, and even the stage of a World's Fair.

Albert's sense of humor and love of pranks showed themselves early. Neighbor and cousin Dean Sturgill recalled Albert and a neighbor boy would often walk the long mountain paths out of Fees Branch to Wolf Knob School together. Sometimes on their walk, they would stop at a neighbor's fenced cow lot and see the cows standing around the haystack, waiting to be fed. "Well, Albert would make sure no one was watching," said Dean, "and climb up on that haystack and throw some hay down to the cattle. The old man who owned the place would come down later and scratch his head. He never could figure out how those cows were gettin' hay from the top of the stack and eatin' their fill!"

Albert was also a noted expert at building something the boys at school called a "dumb bull." He would take a big-size Quaker Oats box and punch a hole in the bottom, in the center. Then he would take a button and tie a string on it and run that string through the hole. The final step was to wax the string with beeswax. Then Albert and his friends would grab that button and pull the string through the box. As Dean Sturgill described it, "That thing would make the bellerin'est, roarin'est noise you ever head! It would sound like a bull up on the hill squallerin'!" If the boys played their "dumb bull" at night, they'd hear shots fired into the air, see barn lanterns light up and stir up the entire community.[12]

Albert spent his younger teen years at home and school when he could make it, helping with the family chores and watching his younger brother, Ernest. During this time, the beginnings of the Great Depression and the start of World War II took its toll on an already impoverished area. Food, clothing, and anything resembling leisure time pursuits were hard to come by but essential to daily life in the mountains. Albert became more and more resourceful. Besides building fiddles in the barn, Albert became an incessant whittler.

Whenever he finished the chores he could be found on the porch or on a stump in the yard using his trusty pocketknife to carve just about anything. He carved little mice, birds' nests with baby birds, frogs, wagons and carts and a variety of livestock that delighted his younger brother and all of his neighbors. He became very adept at using a pocketknife to whittle all sorts of whimsical creatures, many of which would also later adorn the headstocks of his famous fiddles.

If Albert could "see it in my head," he could carve it, he told one reporter. "As long as I had time, I would carve wood, you know and make all kinds of things and all kinds of little mechanical things," he said. "I'd carve frogs and mice and birds and just anything that come along, skulls. I carved a skull of buckeye one time, of white wood. It was a pretty weird looking thing and I decided, it looked so good and all that, I'd, ah, its jaws needed work all the time and I fixed that thing up with a set of old clock works. A little wire running out of them so that it would keep that thing's jaws a biting all the time."[13]

Albert often had more time to whittle on fiddles, toys and projects than his brothers because, according to his own accounts, "I wasn't too strong, so they'd leave me at the house lots of time to do the housework." In addition, running a farm and a household full of four boys often took its toll on his mother and she was sick a lot and needed to be cared for. This would establish a pattern that Albert would follow for the rest of his mother's long life, working, carving, and caring for Della Mae.[14]

Doctors in the mountains were hard to come by. Usually families just dealt with illness as best they could, relying on passed-down home remedies and the almanac for medical intervention. Albert remembered, for example, that when he got what they called "the croup" or laryngitis, his mother would kill a skunk and render the fat from the outside of the skunk's body and cook it down to make an oil out of it. Then "she'd either put some sugar in a spoon with it and make you swallow it, or someone would put a knee in your stomach and hold your hair back and when you hollered they'd pour that oil down you."

Mothers like Albert's frequently worried about their children having worms, which could be deadly, so another remedy of his mother's was "Worm Seed." She would use the seed of the weed called Jerusalem oak and mix it with molasses and periodically force Albert and his brothers

Two—An Appalachian Upbringing

to take large doses. "If anybody'd got sick and they poured a pint of that down you, you'd have died anyhow," Albert laughed.

Albert also recalled collecting resin off of balsam pine trees for his mother's use. "It was awful good medicine," he recalled. He also recalled his mother putting onions out on windowsills around the house to "draw the germs out," especially during the threat of typhoid epidemics. She also used onions to make poultices whenever one of her sons had a bad chest cold.

Della Mae worried that Albert, who was always a bit smaller than her other boys and seemed to be susceptible to viruses and other ailments, needed to be protected. That afforded him a lot of time to work on his projects and to develop his skills.

"They'd leave me at the house," said Albert, "and after I'd get the housework done, I'd hit out under an apple tree or something, you know, and carve something. Sometimes it was fiddles, or it'd be some wood carving or something." As Albert carved and whittled, his skill became refined and both his fiddles and his carvings became something to be treasured by friends and family. By the time he was 15, Albert had built at least three fiddles and carved countless animals. All of this had been done with a pocketknife and various hand tools, as electricity wasn't available.[15]

One day, as a young teen, Albert decided that since his brothers had gone off to work, and he was all alone with chores done, he needed to have a guitar player who would stay around the house with him. He had been learning guitar from his brothers and knew the chords and string positions. He started examining the guitar and decided he would do something about his dilemma.

He built a rack to put the guitar in and then designed some levers to push down the strings in chord forms. Then he rigged a pick on a shaft that he could operate up and down with his left foot, and suddenly he could play the guitar and the fiddle at the same time! "After I got them both going at once, I could keep time with myself there, you know," said Albert, "and I could play that thing right along. It'd play good, you know." One can only imagine what Albert's brothers thought when they came in from work, seeing Albert playing both the fiddle and guitar at once.[16]

As Albert moved to Mt. Rogers High School, he often stayed at the home of his great uncle because the trip across the mountain from his home was just too far. George Finley lived alone just above the schoolhouse and welcomed Albert's help around his small farm. He was a tall, lean and thin man, up into his years, but he had been playing mountain fiddle for most of his years. In exchange for Albert's help around the farm, George took time to teach Albert many of the old tunes he had collected over the years, tunes that had been in the region since before the Civil War.

Although George was too old to play out much anymore, he delighted in Albert's interest in his tunes and stories and patiently showed Albert his bowing style and shared his immense memory of tunes. But Albert would always have to coax him to get his fiddle down. "Oh, I can't play no more," he'd tell Albert. "The rheumatism's got me." But sooner or later, Albert would win out. Still tucking his fiddle into his vest, his long moustache teasing the end of the bow, the old man and the high-schooler would sit on the porch or in the living room after school, playing the old tunes of Whitetop Mountain.

"I don't think I ever heard a better fiddler at anytime," Albert recalled. "He was a single note fiddler, never hit a chord, clean and crisp." Albert remembered that the only time he heard his great uncle play on two strings was when he used one as a "drone" to accompany the melody. "He'd play tunes like Bonaparte's Retreat and just raise the hair on your head with that drone string on there. He could play Forked Deer, and Arkansas Traveler, and all of 'em you know."

Albert paid careful attention to his great uncle's playing. "I was my own worst critic," he recalled, "because I wanted to get it right. I wanted to play those tunes the way they were supposed to be played here."

Whitter and Hash

After playing many schoolhouse dances with his friends and playing out at house parties with his brothers, Albert had begun to project a fiddling style that very much resembled that of his favorite fiddler, G.B. Grayson of Grayson and Whitter. When Henry Whitter, whose musical partner Grayson had recently passed away, met Albert in the early 1930s, he couldn't believe his good fortune. This young man had just the sound that had made Whitter one of the most famous of the early hillbilly recording artists.

Though Albert had met Whitter at the Whitetop festival, it was his older two brothers who came to him with a report that "Mr. Whitter is looking for a fiddler to play with him full time." Upon hearing that, Albert grabbed his best fiddle and walked 18 miles, over and down Whitetop

Two—An Appalachian Upbringing

Mountain. "I started out in the afternoon and got about halfway, and then stayed with a neighbor down the mountain a ways. I got to his house about 10 in the morning the next day."

Whitter, who remembered Albert, opened the door and said, "Come on in, we'll tune up here and see if I can play with you."

Albert remembered that day very well. "We started playing and played and I began to wonder if we was ever going to quit. We played all that day," Albert said. "Then I went off to bed and it wasn't a few hours when he came and woke me up." Whitter wanted Albert to go with him to a party some neighbors were having.

"We got over there," remembered Albert, "and we played all night." When the two finally got home to Whitter's house and Albert got some sleep, Whitter wanted him to play some more, and so they played all the second day. "By the end of that day, I'd had about all I could take," said Albert, "but he was used to it!"

Whitter was a Grayson County native, born in nearby Carroll County in 1892. He had developed his musical abilities while working at the Washington Mill, in Fries, Virginia, along the banks of the New River, where he had become something of a local phenomenon, often being asked to play at parties by the mill bosses. He had grown up playing harmonica and guitar anywhere he could find an audience, at work, at home, often drawing crowds to his front porch, and on the streets of Grayson County. By 1926, Whitter had met and recorded for Ralph Peer, the famed New York talent scout who single handedly orchestrated the famous sessions in Bristol. He had been paid to travel to Peer's New York studio and had successfully wowed the hillbilly recording entrepreneur.

Of the 36 sides that Whitter had recorded for Peer's New York–based label, one, "The Wreck of the Old 97," had become nationally known. Another, "New River Train," first recorded by Whitter in 1924, was to become a national standard in both old-time and bluegrass circles. Because of this success he was also invited to and attended the famed Bristol Sessions where he recorded two numbers. However, both tunes were harmonica numbers and never gained the attention that his ballads did, although today they are revered as early examples of the blues harmonica style. Whitter would not remain a solo act for long.

In 1927, shortly after the Bristol recordings, he met G.B. Grayson at the Mountain City Fiddler's Convention in Tennessee. Almost immediately the two immensely talented musicians became a duo, Grayson's accomplished and driving fiddle style adding emphasis to Whitter's growing collection of ballads and songs about rural life in the Blue Ridge. During their short three years together, they recorded about 38 sides for Victor records, many of which would become legendary. Included among their recordings were "Tom Dooley," "Handsome Molly," "Short Life of Trouble," "Train 45," "I've Always Been a Rambler" and others that would later become bluegrass, folk and country standards.

In 1930, their remarkable collaboration came to an abrupt end. Hitchhiking from Damascus, Virginia, to his home five miles down the road in Laurel Bloomery, Tennessee, Grayson threw his fiddle into the back of a friend's car and gladly jumped on the running boards of the over-full vehicle. While crossing a bridge just out of Damascus, the driver lost control of the car and Grayson plunged to his death.[17]

Albert Hash had loved Grayson's playing and routinely listened to his music on the Victrola, but he had never met him, even though he had grown up just a few miles over Whitetop Mountain from him. "The barrier was the mountains. There was no transportation, only a horse," said Albert. It would have been a three-day journey by horseback to visit Grayson in Tennessee, so Albert had to carefully dissect his playing, note for note, from the Victrola.

At the time Albert went to see him, Whitter was living in Crumpler, North Carolina, on the Virginia border. "He was a very likeable fellow," said Albert, "a nice man, and he liked the way I played." Whitter was so impressed that he invited Albert to come live with him in Crumpler for a while and help him make another musical go at it as his fiddling partner. Apparently Albert sounded so much like Grayson that Whitter asked him to play shows with him across the region and presented Albert with a fiddle that he himself had built and asked him to play it on the tour.[18]

Henry Whitter owned a Model A Ford, purchased with his recording royalties, and teenaged Albert hadn't learned how to drive, so he rode with Whitter to shows over rutted, muddy mountain roads to Chilhowie, Damascus and Marion, Virginia, and on down to Bristol, Tennessee. Not only was Albert just learning to drive and not confident at it, but Mr. Whitter had a nervous condition, caused by diabetes, that interfered with his eyesight and his ability to react. Often, Albert would have to grab the wheel to avoid an oncoming car or to keep from sailing off the road and down a mountain. He often clenched his jaw as they sailed up and down the highest mountains in Virginia, swerving and jumping from edge to edge.

"I was reluctant to go with him," Albert recalled in an interview, "because he wouldn't see a car until it was right at you, and it would scare

Two—An Appalachian Upbringing

Henry Whitter (*left*) **and Albert Hash on the porch of Whitter's home in Healing Springs, North Carolina (courtesy of Brian and Ann Baker Forehand).**

him almost to death and he'd run his car plumb off the road to dodge that. Something was eatin' on him in some way or other, so his vision didn't work, or he wouldn't concentrate on what was comin' up in front of him and it was pitiful," he said.

Despite Henry Whitter's driving habits, Albert truly enjoyed playing with the songster and liked his company. "He treated me like I was his own boy, and we had a good time together," Albert said. During this time, Hash and Whitter had their own posters and would personalize them to the school or hall they were playing. They even put the posters up themselves. They did their own booking, advertising, and managing. After a year of travelling the area with Whitter, Albert had enough of perilous drives and decided to seek work elsewhere. However, the professional experience of playing packed concert halls and school gymnasiums with one of America's best-known songsters was invaluable to the young man and gave him the confidence he needed to become a seasoned stage performer.[19]

Fiddlin' Years

After high school, Albert lived mostly at home caring for his mother and spent a lot of his time building fiddles, honing his fiddling skills, and playing for gatherings throughout the region. He played house parties and box suppers at the school, with Gaither Farmer, a neighbor, backing him up as well as other locals like E.C. Ball and E.C.'s brother-in-law, Wade Reedy. Since living room dances were easily organized, Albert found himself in great demand as a dance fiddler:

> We used to have a dance at somebody's house nearly every week. There was not anything much for entertainment other than things [like] dances and music and we just made good use of that. And we'd go to a house, say like this 'un, with no more room than I have here, maybe 12 by 20 feet and there wouldn't be a whole big crowd like there would be at a dance hall. There'd be alot of people there, but not too many would dance anyhow, just come over to hear the music and so on. They'd just pick up the furniture and move it out of the way and set here over in the corner and there it went. Girls on one side of the house and boys on the other. Yeah—played for thousands of them.[20]

Albert's mother and other parents carefully supervised these parties, but not too carefully. "They would usually sit back and paid no attention to you, you know. They'd talk among themselves and it would be just a good social gathering, no trouble. No, nothing to bother anybody. Everybody behaved and everybody had a good time," he said.[21]

Besides dances, Albert often found himself playing for corn shuckings in the late summer. Not all of those events were without some serious frivolity. "Now there was some that enjoyed a sip or two of that good mountain liquor," remembered Albert. "They'd pile that corn up in a great big pile, 10 feet high and as wide as this room. Then someone would put a jug of moonshine right in the middle of that pile and the first person to shuck into that got to take the first drink. You shoulda seen those husks fly!"

As Albert turned 20, he headed to Franklin D. Roosevelt's Civilian Conservation Corps (CCC), looking for work like many young men his

Two—An Appalachian Upbringing

age including his brothers. This was his first paying job outside of the food and money he sometimes made for playing music on his own. The CCC camp he worked at was located in Baywood, Virginia. While his brothers labored with stone and construction, the slighter, weaker Albert was assigned to KP duty. As soon as the cooks found out that Albert could fiddle, he was assigned to be the camp's resident musician and he played regularly for not only the cooks but for all of the workers as they had their lunch. Albert literally fiddled his time away on the job. The CCC folks, who had a penchant for employing not just workers but also artists and craftsmen, loved the idea of Albert's lunchtime shows so much that they hired musicians at other camps as well.[22]

During that time, Albert developed a keen interest in a young woman he had met in high school, Ms. Ethel Ruth Spencer. Ethel was the granddaughter of famed dancer Uncle Bud Spencer and came from a musical family in the Fees Branch area of Grayson. Ethel's father, Orie, played the fiddle and danced. Although Ethel could play the pump organ, she rarely played with Albert. She loved most to dance with Albert when she could pry the fiddle out of his hands or coax him out to a dance where he wasn't the fiddler. Albert courted her through his 20s, bringing her along to dances and performances throughout the area. Not having a long-term job and having to live at home made it hard for him to consider marriage, but he and Ethel formed a deep, powerful bond.

"She was a dancer," Albert told researchers from Appalachian State University. "I hardly ever did get to dance with her, that's why I can't dance to this day, but I always did manage to walk her home. I had to fiddle until I was ready to fall out of the chair while she had a good time a-dancin'. But, I enjoyed every minute of it." Albert described playing at corn shuckings while neighbors husked huge piles of corn and going to play at bean stringings, apple cuttings and molasses boiling parties.

Ethel danced to his fiddling and to the music of the many bands Albert played in during this time. She danced in a local Blue Ridge style called "flat footing" that often resembled a hybrid of Irish step-dancing and Cherokee pageant dancing. Albert's bands at this time involved many different local players, and none of these groups could really afford studio work, however some recorded documentation exists from the early 1940s and a few recordings, some made at furniture stores, exist.

"I just picked up fellers here and there," described Albert. "I'd just get my bands together." Among the bands he built was the original Whitetop Mountain Band, with Dent Blevins on mandolin and Frank and Henry

Blevins and Archie Finlay on guitars. Albert, of course, played fiddle. A bit later he joined up with a band from Taylor's Valley, Virginia, called the Spice Bottom Boys. This band featured a local favorite, John Yates, on guitar and Lon Hill, a bluegrass style banjo player. "My type is traditional, but I could play that bluegrass if I needed to," commented Albert.

After the Spice Bottom Boys, he played with more of a country and western style setup in a band called the Carolina Troubadours. They were from North Carolina and featured Dean Hart on bass, Jim Poe (who Albert would have a long musical collaboration with) on a flat top Martin guitar, and lead singer Clay Wilson. To capture the country and western audience, they also featured an electric steel guitar played by Brian Adams. Albert would perform with this band on and off for several years, playing for two state governors and many dignitaries in Ashe County, North Carolina, where the band was a hit.

He recorded at least two sides, "Ragtime Annie" and "Wabash Cannonball," with Archie Finlay on guitar and Dent Blevins on banjo during this time. He also recorded two other sides, possibly at a furniture store showroom, with the Blevins brothers, Frank, Henry and Dent. These recordings include "Cabin Home on the Hill" and "Will You Be Loving Another Man?"[23] Three of the four songs recorded during this time are representative of the emerging bluegrass genre that was beginning to sweep through the mountains, led by Bill Monroe and his Bluegrass Boys, but Albert's repertoire mainly consisted of old-time fiddle tunes learned locally or through recordings.

Starting a Family of His Own

As the war in Europe loomed and things got even tighter financially in the mountains, Albert decided, with his brothers Rhudy and Ernest, to head north to look for work. They landed near Washington, D.C., in Arlington, Virginia. Albert had been turned down for active service because of a mild heart condition (like many Appalachian hill folk his age, he was a heavy smoker which probably exacerbated his condition). He resisted at first, but the tightness of the job market and the necessity of having a career and a nest egg to finance his marriage convinced Albert that working in Arlington's naval yard to build torpedoes would be a form of alternative service.

He had written back to Ethel, initially in November of 1943, "I could

Two—An Appalachian Upbringing

get on at the torpedo plant here, but they won't give a Xmas bonus, and that don't suit me at all. I won't have that kind of job." After trying to get several jobs in Silver Spring, Maryland, he evidently changed his mind about the torpedo plant, writing in May of 1944 from Alexandria: "I like it just fine, it is a good place to make money and the people are the Southern type. I make 87 and ½ cents an hour, six days a week. Thousands of men work here."[24]

The "bomb factory," as Albert often referred to it, afforded Albert another opportunity: He could train to be a machinist. Considered by the factory staff a "machinist in training," Albert was enamored with the opportunity. His Blue Ridge ingenuity and his homegrown sensibility lent itself perfectly to the task. By 1944, Albert felt so comfortable in his new career that he returned home to Fees Branch and asked Ethel to become his wife.

They were married on January 17, 1944. Evidently, the preacher Albert chose to perform the service was sick in bed, and there wasn't another one available for miles. So Albert convinced the preacher to perform the ceremony from his bed, with he and Ethel standing to the side. He found a small place for them to begin their lives together in Alexandria. They stayed until the end of the war.

Albert and Ethel at their small home in Arlington, Virginia, in 1944, before moving back to the mountains (courtesy Carla Osborne).

Appalachian Fiddler Albert Hash

In 1945, Albert, homesick for the mountains, decided to take Ethel back to the Blue Ridge. They rented a small place just over the border from Virginia, again in Fees Branch, North Carolina, where he had spent his earliest years, and Albert decided to try his hand at farming. "I bought me a hoe and a bag of fertilizer," recounted Albert. "I had a little place back up on the head of this creek that runs over here and I went up there and pretended to raise a crop of corn. I picked more blackberries than anything!"[25]

That year, Albert and Ethel's first daughter, Joyce Mae, was born and the couple worked hard to build a loving, caring home for her. They were able to pay for the doctor with money Albert had saved while working at the torpedo plant. However, four years later, in 1949, when their second daughter, Audrey Marie, was born, Albert's farming had not benefited them any cash on hand and paying for the doctor was a different story.

So Albert, toiling late hours in his shop, built a beautiful fiddle with a Native American figure on the head (his first human likeness on a fiddle, which would later become his trademark) and a colorful inlay on the back. The day after Audrey was born, having just finished the fiddle, Albert walked the 20 miles into the town of Jefferson, North Carolina, and

Albert and Ethel with their daughters, ca. 1955. From left, Joyce Mae Hash, Audrey Marie Hash, Ethel and Albert (courtesy Carla Osborne).

found a buyer for the fiddle to pay for the hospital bill. While he was in town, he bought some material with blue flowers on it with money left over from the sale of the fiddle. He went home and figured out how to sew Ethel a dress so that she would have something nice to wear home from the hospital.

This was not an easy birth for Ethel so Albert's gift must've meant a lot. When Ethel knew the baby was on its way, the closest car that could get them the 20 miles to the hospital was two miles down a path from their house and the old rutted road was not passable. Ethel had to be laid on a sled and hauled down the mountain behind a horse just to get to a car that could take her into Lansing.

Years later, Albert would often tease his youngest daughter by saying, "That was a raw deal. I got the bad end of it, trading that beautiful fiddle for this scrawny little runt of a girl!" Some of Audrey and Joyce Mae's earliest memories would be rocking on their mother's lap listening to E.C. and Orna Ball or other local musicians playing in their parlor with their dad.[26]

Farming and Fiddlin'

Albert and Ethel tried farming in a couple of places in North Carolina and Virginia over the next 10 years, but they both soon realized that Albert was no farmer. During this time, to supplement his income, Albert began a new hobby, repairing guns and making gunstocks for people. He enjoyed carving custom stocks for rifles and pistols and local folks were delighted to have someone who could repair their guns. In Fees Branch, just over the line in North Carolina, Albert tried to resurrect his family's homestead, working at farming during the day and playing and building fiddles at night and on the weekend.

During this time, in the late '40s and early '50s, Albert and Ethel established themselves as neighbors whose door was always open, and he loved to encourage young people to come and play. Fiddler Dean Sturgill remembered that as a young man, around 1950, he would travel from Spencer Branch over the mountain to Albert's place on Fees Branch. He would sometimes travel with his brother Breece. They'd take off right after supper and stay as late as they could at Albert's, yearning to play the fiddle like the young master Albert had become. They would always be greeted with "Hi, young 'un" as they came in the door, often cold and hungry. They'd often be fed by Ethel and be encouraged to play along.

Appalachian Fiddler Albert Hash

Fiddler and poet Dean Sturgill, November 2017 (photograph by Jim Kacsmarik).

Later, Dean became a renowned area fiddler and his brother became an instrument maker, both learning their craft from Albert. Dean immortalized those trips to see Albert in this poem he wrote.

The Fiddler of Fees Branch
by Dean Sturgill (used by permission of the author)

We waded through the snows of winter,
When no winter moon shone,
And walked through the storms of summer
to get to his home.
Forty years ago, the Fees Branch fiddler was young and thin,
He'd say, "Come in, youngins,' how have you youngins' been?"
He'd say, "I'm doin' very well, I reckon. Able to totter about!"
He'd pull Prince Albert from his pocket, and take some Prince Albert out.
With cigarette rolled and lighted, he'd settle back in his seat,
To rest his worn back and to rest his weary feet.
We knew that with Ax or cradle, he'd toiled all day
But sooner or later, we'd ask him to play.
He'd take the fiddle from the wall and pick and tune the strings and say,
"Boys, don't play much anymore, can't do much with the thing."
His fiddle was a fiddle of beauty,
of spruce and curly maple, handmade.
On the back an engraved peacock of many colors with many jewels inlaid.

Two—An Appalachian Upbringing

The scroll was the head of an eagle; mean eyes looked every way,
A fingerboard of Emory, with flowers of mother of pearl inlay.
He played the fiddle under his chin, on his head, behind his back,
Big-eyed backwoods booger boys never seen anything like that.
The Cacklin' Hen cackled, and the Red Rooster Crowed,
As the Fees Branch Fiddler sawed strings with his bow.
To the Arkansas Traveller the boys listened while the lamplight danced,
And love, mystery and mastery of the fiddle and fiddler were enhanced.
He played "I held her by Her Little Brown Hand," and put the bow away.
Through the snows of winter and storms of summer back home we would go.
With summertime over, milkin' done, again to Fees Branch we would dash,
Because the Fees Branch fiddler was the great Albert Hash.
Forty years later the great Fees Branch fiddler is gone,
But the Fees Branch fiddler didn't leave us alone.
Today beside the falling waters of Fees Branch the spring birds still sing,
And the resounding sound of
  the Fees Branch fiddler's
  fiddle still rings.[27]

Dean also recalled hiking up Fees Branch to Albert and Ethel's house one night during a rainstorm with his brother, hoping to hear some great tunes. When they arrived at Albert's already drenched, Ethel helped them out of their wet coats and set them on the couch in the living room where Albert had already taken down his fiddle. "He played so great that night," recalled Dean. "We hung on every note."

Happy, and full of tunes in their heads as well as some of Ethel's cooking in their bellies, Dean and his brother headed back over the ridges and hollers to their home. When they came to a clearing on the side of a mountain, the storm abruptly halted and the clouds quickly cleared. "At the same time the

Albert and an unknown banjo player, 1964 (courtesy Carla Osborne).

stars came out that moment, so did thousands of lightning bugs," recalled Dean.

It was a powerful moment that Dean has never forgotten—the tunes in his head, the storm clearing and the night forest lit up with the twinkling of one of the largest flights of fireflies the boys had ever seen. "There was something about that night, the mountains and the light," he said, "that made the importance of Albert's music stick with me forever."

Thornton Learns to Fiddle

Ethel Hash had a much younger brother, Thornton Spencer, who was born in 1935, the same year as his cousin Dean. At about the age of 11, Thornton began to spend every spare minute at Albert's house. His favorite place to sit was in Albert's shop, where he would spend hours watching Albert work. What most caught Thornton's eye, however, were the fiddles that Albert had hanging on the wall.

One day Thornton pulled down a fiddle off the bench and just started to saw on it. When Albert heard him playing, he said, "You know, I think you could learn how to play that. And I'll tell you what; I've got to go out of town for a week, to go visit my brothers" (Ernest and Rhudy, who had moved to Appomattox). "I'm gonna show you two tunes on that thing. If you learn them by the time I come back, I'll give you that fiddle to keep." Before he left, Albert carefully showed Thornton "Ragtime Annie" and "Chicken Reel."

Thornton couldn't believe his good fortune. He took that fiddle home and practiced those two tunes, day and night, for a week. When he heard Albert was back, Thornton ran breathlessly to Albert's house and started to play. A surprised Albert looked up to see who was fiddling. A wide smile overtook him, and he looked with pride at Thornton and told him, "You better take good care of that new fiddle you earned."[28] Those two tunes, Thornton's first, would later become signature tunes for Thornton. He played them nearly every performance until his death in 2017.

Thornton also knew the guitar and became a fixture at Albert and Ethel's house, often spending the night. Thornton was a quick learner and was soon playing much of Albert's repertoire, either backing Albert on guitar or twin fiddling with his brother-in-law. This was the beginning of what would, in later years, become the nationally famous Whitetop Mountain Band.

Two—An Appalachian Upbringing

According to his cousin Dean Sturgill, Thornton very rarely wore short-sleeved shirts. Thousands of photos taken of Thornton in his later life showed him in his most familiar garb, a long-sleeve, button-down shirt, often black. According to Dean, this was because of a day they spent together in a hay field when they were young men. A neighbor was feeling ill and having trouble getting his hay in from the field, so Thornton's dad, Orlie, corralled several of the teen boys in the area to help.

"Thornton showed up in a white t-shirt, short-sleeved," said Dean. Nearly everybody else had long-sleeve shirts on. Anyone who has baled hay and tossed the bales into a cart and then into a hay barn knows that hay irritates the skin and often causes welts to rise on bare skin. By the end of that day, Thornton's arms and neck were covered with painful, itching welts. As far as anyone recollects, he rarely wore a short-sleeved shirt from that day on.[29]

Perhaps more important, this story points out the fierce sense of community that Albert, Thornton, Dean and others who grew up and lived in the shadows of Virginia's highest mountains often felt. When a neighbor called and told you that someone needed help, it was your duty to respond.

The Fees Branch Neighbor

During his time trying his hand at farming on Fees Branch, Albert was already considered to be a reliable gentleman in the community and someone that neighbors often relied on to help solve problems. One day, some neighbors approached Albert with the news that one of the residents of another community across the creek had lost a child. It seems that two small children had been playing with a gun that had discharged, killing one of the kids. The head of the family was a woman considered to be what the locals referred to as an "old rip," or a woman of the night.

Albert, wanting to do what he could to help, stopped at a neighbor's farm and recruited the man of the house to accompany him to the woman's home. When they entered the home, Albert observed many children of various ages running about. The woman of the house told Albert and his neighbor to put their coats on the bed. When they entered the bedroom, they saw a small child laid out on the bed, motionless. They both assumed the poor thing was the dead child and hadn't been buried.

Albert talked to her about making preparations for the child and where she might bury him. He also called the sheriff for her and did what he could to calm her down. As he entered the bedroom to get his coat to leave, the child on the bed rolled over and bounced right off the bed. The child, who had been sleeping, startled Albert so badly that he could barely catch his breath. Some 60 years later, neighbors are still telling the story.[30]

Back to Town

After realizing he wasn't meant to be a farmer, Albert decided to use his skills as a machinist and applied for work at Sprague Electric in Lansing, Ashe County, not far from Fees Branch. In 1955 he and Ethel rented a small home across from the high school in Lansing and established themselves in their new neighborhood—in town, for a change.

This new job, as a machinist, suited Albert perfectly. He was given a very large machine shop to work in that was well equipped and the company treated him well. "I had a lot of ambition and I was a lot younger," Albert remembered, "so I didn't take any breaks. I'd get there early of the morning and leave late and sometimes I'd go in on a Saturday and they'd allow me to make something for myself, and they was awful good that way," he said.[31]

In his Saturday free time at the plant he began to make guns, lots and lots of guns. Mostly he built handguns, copying legendary styles like the Frontier Colt that won the West. Albert also began to experiment with working on clocks and became enamored with their inner workings and mechanisms. He became so fascinated that he decided he needed to learn mechanical engineering. At this point, this former poor mountain boy, who had only a high school education, enrolled in an engineering class through the mail and began to spend nights poring through mechanical engineering textbooks after working nine-hour days.

Albert's engineering projects started to take over his home. When he realized he needed more room to work than their small Lansing home across from the high school afforded, Albert found an old abandoned school bus, dragged it in front of the house near the road, and outfitted it with a small kerosene heater, removed the seats and began to install his machines, inventions, and woodworking projects. It also doubled as a fiddle-building shop.

As Albert's new career challenged him and his girls grew to be school aged, he did what many mountain musicians do: He put the music and instrument building aside to focus on making his family secure. While the nearby Whitetop Mountain still loomed large in his life, he had to focus on his job, his children and the woman he so dearly loved. For a few years, music would take a backseat.

Three

Clocks, Machines and "Govn'ment Work"

Albert quickly won favor with his Sprague managers and coworkers. His ability to envision a project and then take action became revered at the plant. Often, a supervisor or engineer would come into his machine shop and bring a detailed blueprint for Albert to look at. Albert would ask him to describe the machine or part, its function, and its size.

As soon as the supervisor or engineer was done and left him to it, he would tear up the blueprint and go to work, building exactly what had been described or building a version of it with his own innovations. Sometimes he would build a small working model just to make sure it was what the engineer had envisioned before he built the full-sized machine. The engineers were amazed at the skill and the speed with which Albert did his work.

In the late 1950s and 1960s, Sprague was a leader in making electric semiconductors and capacitors. The company had been founded in the 1920s in Massachusetts, and the Lansing plant was a part of its worldwide growth. The new Lansing plant employed hundreds of workers at its height in the 1950s and '60s and became a major economic engine in this remote North Carolina town.

Sprague had been both a consumer product manufacturer and a major military supplier of electronics in World War II, helping to develop sophisticated bomb ignition systems as well as leading the burgeoning miniaturization movement in electronics. The Lansing plant was part of its strategy to capture a sizeable chunk of the post-war electronics market, focusing on capacitors and transistors and eventually the emerging computer market.

Three—Clocks, Machines and "Govn'ment Work"

The Corporate Jester

Albert's sense of humor quickly became evident to his coworkers at Sprague and eventually became legendary. For example, he noticed that many of his superiors had very fancy plaques on their desks announcing their name and company rank, such as "Vice President of Finance" or "Floor Supervisor." Not wanting to be outdone, Albert one day took the side of his toolbox and a tube of silver resin used for capacitors and carefully crafted a plaque of his own. It read "Mr. Hash, Rectumologist." It sat on his workbench until the plant nurse came by and saw it, and then Albert, more than a bit embarrassed, scrubbed it off.[1]

Albert quickly became an asset to the company, designing many machines that automated some of the more mundane tasks on the Sprague assembly line and keeping many machines up and running. Albert was friendly with everyone at Sprague, except the engineers. "For some reason, he didn't have much time for the engineering staff," Jerry Smith, a former member of the Sprague engineering team, told us. "Somehow, though, he took a liking to me."

When Albert's supervisors noticed that he and Jerry seemed to get along, they assigned Jerry to watch what Albert was designing and building for the company and to make schematics and blueprints of his creations. That way, they could replicate Albert's work at other plants. "Hardest job I ever had," he said, "trying to keep up with everything Albert was doing and creating." Jerry enjoyed working with Albert and the two became fast friends. They would remain friends for the rest of Albert's life.[2]

Albert's genius at machine work was very different from that of his coworkers. "I always told the boys in the shop that I was training, 'I build it upstairs [pointing to his head] first.' I can see that thing before I ever start to work on it, I can see it working," he said.

Albert went on to say, "I have always worked a different method from most every other machinist that I have worked with. They would want to make sketches and drawings and compare to this to this and so on. I would never make them like that. When the plant manager would come and ask me, lots of times he'd come over the top of my foreman and ask me directly if I could make a machine to do a certain job. I always had the answer ready for him. Yes sir."

At that point, Albert would wander off to the coffee pot and then sit down and ponder the new machine. "I would begin to say, 'Now this will work this way, buy why won't it work this way. I would pick out the reasons why it will work and why it won't work," he explained. "And when I got the reasons why it would work all together and I had no more reasons why it wouldn't work, I would start machining out pieces and piling them up in a pile."

This approach appeared to drive Albert's bosses crazy. They would try to follow him around the plant and figure out what he was doing, but it seemed to make no logical sense. He often came into the shop to find his boss trying to assemble the parts he had machined into something, always to no avail. When his boss gave up trying to make it work, Albert would methodically assemble the parts into a machine, put it on a truck and take it out to the assembly line and put it to work, no test runs or trials needed.

"Very few times have I ever made a piece of machinery that was a flop, you know," Albert recalled. "It all worked out because I wouldn't start until I had it figured out that it would work."[3]

Albert's pranks became legendary at Sprague. One day, a young woman who operated a machine that Albert built sent word to Albert that the machine wasn't working. Albert grabbed his toolbox and headed to the department where she worked in the plant. While Albert was diagnosing the problem, and the woman had gone to the restroom, a young man who knew Albert and worked in close proximity to the young woman approached.

"May I ask you a question?" the young man asked.

"OK," said Albert, still working.

"That young woman who works here is awful pretty," he said to Albert. "Do you think she'd go out with me?"

"Well, she might," said Albert with a serious look. "I'll tell you what, when she and the kids and I are having dinner tonight, let me ask her."

The young man backed away from Albert to his workstation as quickly as he could. Albert, who didn't really know the woman at all, chuckled quietly to himself. Those who had seen the prank could not contain themselves and nearly doubled over in laughter.[4]

Albert's "Laboratory"

Over the next several years, Albert worked at Sprague as Ethel spent much of her time raising their two daughters. Joyce was frailer than her younger sister and required more of her mother's time. Albert often worried about her, but she turned out to live a good life. She married young,

Three—Clocks, Machines and "Govn'ment Work"

at 16, and became a devoted mother and wife, adopting her father's sense of community and service as well as her mother's sense of commitment to family and friends. Audrey, on the other hand, spent her time hanging out in her father's shop, interested in everything he was doing and building.

In his off hours, in his converted bus shop in front of the high school (that Albert referred to as his "laboratory"), Albert's work interest turned away from fiddle building to a new hobby: clock building and repair. In fact, one visitor to his Lansing house during this phase recalled sitting with the Hash family in the living room when Albert declared, "What time do you suppose it is, Ethel?" Suddenly, Albert's wife rose ceremoniously from her chair and traveled up and down their long mantle, winding the variety of clocks that Albert had built or repaired, causing a cacophony to fill the living room.[5]

"That was another dream of mine," said Albert. "When I was little, we had a neighbor who had a big old clock in the living room. I'd spend the night there with them sometimes and I'd listen to that big old clock 'tic, tock, tic, tic, and so on' and then I'd dream about how it was made."

Albert's curiosity about clocks started with gears. At first, he would just make what he would call "clock works," wooden gears that worked together continuously off of a pendulum and a winder. He expanded that work to build actual clocks. He combined his love of whittling with his machine skills, and all of his clock gears were made of wood. In fact, some of the clocks he owned and worked on, including those he built from scratch, had only wooden parts.

However, as Albert's infatuation with time mechanisms grew, he wanted to make bigger, more sophisticated clocks in his shop. His most prized accomplishment became a very large grandfather clock that he built during his Sprague years. It was the first major project that he made with gears and workings out of brass. The brass he used was only ⅛ of an inch thick, much thinner than most large clock works. He made the clock in the style of the pre–Civil War grandfather clocks and made every component of it, including the hinges for the case and the knob for the door.

A small ship traveled back and forth above the pendulum, keeping time, complete with tin sails and a hand-painted ocean backdrop. Albert loved that clock. "You could come in here and take my refrigerator," said Albert, "or take my stove and I'd say, 'Go ahead if you need to.' But don't take that clock. It needs me and I need it."

Before he began building clocks, Albert read every book he could buy or borrow on the history and design of clocks. During an interview with students from Appalachian State, he gave them a lesson on clock history, taking them back to early Chinese dynasties and through the birth of Christianity:

> We had all kinds, all nationalities of people that made clocks, but most of them were German or Dutch. And they called them … the Pennsylvania clocks, you know, the tall clock. This pendulum, as I understand, was adapted to the clock in about 1630, before they had what was known as the balance bar, this piece swung around and back and around and back, just balanced up there held by a piece of string. And that was one of the early clocks, that was thirteenth century clocks beginning in the thirteenth century in China, I believe it was the origin of that clock.
>
> Well, before that was the water clock, which was a container with a tiny hole at the bottom and another container which caught the water as it leaked out of that and raise this float which read the hour of the day as it raised up, you know. I guess they also had the sun dial and the hour glass and what have you, or a mark on the porch to see when the sun got down to a certain time and it's time to start doing the work up. These people made some fantastic clocks. Their ingenuity was something to really be appreciated.
>
> Now there was one fellow who fastened himself up and stayed for I forgot how many years and he come up with this clock that has the Christ and the disciples and they march around at the time this clock is to strike, you know, and then he has Satan and all kinds of figures that will come out at different times and so on. Things like that people have really gone into clock making in a big way.

Like his fiddles, Albert did not keep track of how many clocks he made or repaired, considering it a labor of love rather than a money-making proposition. "I've kind of lost count of them like my fiddles," he said at one point in his building. "I never try to keep track of anything like that."[6]

Albert's technique confounded many a visitor to his school bus shop. Often, he would start with a case for the clock and then design the gears to fit inside the size of the case. One neighbor entered his shop and asked, "What are you building?" noticing a big wooden case on the floor.

"A grandfather clock," replied Albert.

The neighbor retorted, "Well, it looks all right, but where are you going to get your works?"

"I'm going to build them!" said Albert.

"Well, you better build the works first," said the neighbor, "then build the case."

"If I can build the case, I know I can build the works," Albert told him.

Three—Clocks, Machines and "Govn'ment Work"

He built clocks with one-day movements, eight-day movements and 30-day movements. He was fascinated by the math of it all, carefully figuring the gear ratios needed and the number of teeth required to move them. He used steel, cold rolled steel and brass in his clocks and he made the cases mostly of walnut. Some of them he kept, like the grandfather clock with the ships that was always on display in Albert's living room to be admired by the many musicians, friends and family who came to visit, its precise pendulum a backdrop to all conversations and musical sessions in the Hashes' home.[7]

"Govn'ment" Work

Some days during his work at Sprague Electric, there was downtime, when all the machines in the plant were working well and Albert and his small crew of machinists could take a break. On those days, Albert would gather two or three of his colleagues together, including his engineer friend Jerry Smith and declare to the boys that it was "time for our 'govn'ment'" work. This meant that they were going to use the Sprague machines to have some fun.

One Friday at lunch, Albert sawed a long .22 rifle barrel into four equal lengths and presented each of his three colleagues with one. Intrigued, each of the three men held their short barrels and stared at Albert who carefully went to work on his bench. Each of the three looked over his shoulder as he grabbed brass off one shelf and began to fashion the sheets of metal into something.

"We watched everything he did," said Jerry Smith. "We took notes during our breaks and lunch breaks, and stayed a couple of days behind Albert, and slowed him down with questions." Soon it was evident what Albert and they were building: a small swivel-barrel derringer, the plans for which were coming directly from Albert's mind each week.

"He gave us wood from his clock making to fashion the handle stock out of," recounted Jerry, "and he showed us how to calibrate the pistol and make it work." Then, one day a couple of weeks later, the four men walked out of the Sprague over their lunch break and headed for an open field behind the plant. They put up a small target made out of a piece of wood, and each in turn loaded and fired their new pistols. Each fired with accuracy. More than fifty years later, Jerry Smith's Albert Hash–designed derringer still fires with perfect accuracy.

Building a Hash Fiddle

During this time, as Albert's mother entered her early 40s, she began to experience a variety of health problems and became less and less able to deal with day-to-day life. Possibly from the strain of raising four boys with no resources, from the stress of the Great Depression and mountain subsistence farming, she seemed to just give up. Many said she simply had "the vapors." Ethel and Albert helped care for her, as they would for the next 40 years until her death at age 81. Caring for Della Mae, combined with day-to-day work and tasks and the increasing needs of two

Albert, Ethel, and Albert's mother, Della Mae Long Reedy, ca. 1965 (courtesy Carla Osborne).

Three—Clocks, Machines and "Govn'ment Work"

school-aged daughters, kept Albert's fiddle mostly hanging on the wall. He only got it down for the occasional visitor or visits from tune collectors.

He did manage to build a few fiddles during the Sprague years. After his father had rewarded Albert with the fiddle he earned for staying in school, Albert played it until he was in his teens. He had gushed over its beautiful varnish and sleek lines, but his mother had said to him at the time, "Albert, someday you'll make better fiddles than that one." She was right.

Once in high school he had learned enough about the fiddle to know that he didn't like the sound of that store-bought fiddle. He treasured it because it had been the most meaningful gift his father had given him, but he knew he couldn't afford a better one. If he wanted a better fiddle, he'd have to build it.

By the time he went to work at Sprague, he had perfected the ins and outs of fiddle building, including extremely fine finishing and adjusting them for sound. Though he wasn't as prolific at fiddle building as he would be in his later years, Albert built many fine instruments, mostly for himself or close friends, during this time. He expanded his collection of tools and machines and part of his shop was always dedicated to his instrument building and repair. He also began to give his fiddles names instead of numbering them, which makes it very hard to track the number of fiddles that he made. The "laboratory" outside his house now contained clockworks and gun works as well as instruments in various states of completion or repair.

Albert described to one young interviewer the manner in which he created fiddles, hoping the young man, Edwin Lacy, who was interviewing Albert for a high school project, would take up the craft.

> I'll get a piece of wood first for my back plate. I like to use curly maple for the back, and I'll cut it down to ⅝ of an inch thick. And for the top plate is always spruce and I cut it about ⅝ of an inch thick or a little thinner. Then I cut out the blank that looks like a fiddle out of that. Then I begin to form the arch, which is the bulge on the outside, you know.
>
> By cuttin' away the ends of it, cutting it down to where it's around 3/16 of an inch, at the edges, and [not in the middle,] that leaves it round on the back. That has to be carved. A lot of people are under the impression that's steamed and bent in there, but it's not. That arch has to be carved both in your back and your top.
>
> When I go to make the side pieces, I bend them. They're thin, a little less than ⅙ of an inch thick, and I bend them over a hot soldering iron. You just wet one side of those, the side you're going to leave inside the fiddle. You just put that against that hot soldering iron and it'll bend a little. Then move it on down a little farther and it'll bend again. You do this all the way around to match the shape of

Appalachian Fiddler Albert Hash

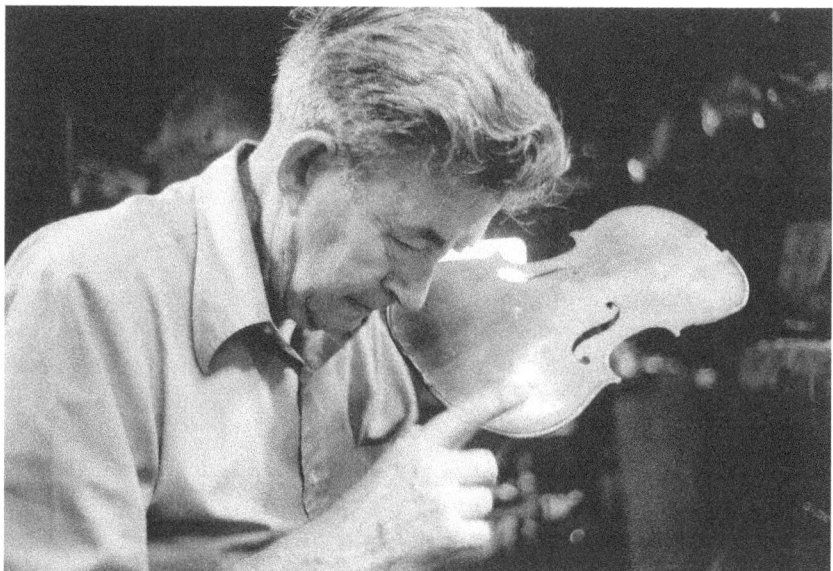

Undated photograph of Albert fine-tuning a fiddle top in his shop (photograph by Mark Sanderford).

the top and bottom. Those sides are in six pieces. They go together at these "C" shapes in here and they go together at the endpin and the neck. Now you can use a one- or two-piece back. You almost always use a two-piece top, so that it will look symmetrical, your grain and the wood. You want parallel grain for your top, it don't matter so much about the back, you can slab cut grain, you know, cut on the slab for the back. But the top must be quarter sawed, so it'll give you a good strong top that way. Then I use ebony or rosewood trimmings on it for fingerboards, the tailpiece and the pegs.[8]

To make it a signature Albert Hash fiddle, though, it needed to have a couple more important elements. "A little trademark that I have is that little peacock that I carve in the back of it. And then it needs a parrot head or some kind of head I carve up on the top to replace the conventional scroll. And then instead of putting the perfoiling around the edges which is three pieces of wood, two of ebony and one of holly, I bind the edge and sides, just like a guitar. That's much better, it don't let the wood break away from you and it don't weaken your instrument," Albert described. "Now that there is an Albert Hash Fiddle!"

Albert was often offered more than $1,500 for one of his fiddles, particularly the one he was playing at the time. Albert did not believe in asking such exorbitant prices for his fiddles because he did not think a real

Three—Clocks, Machines and "Govn'ment Work"

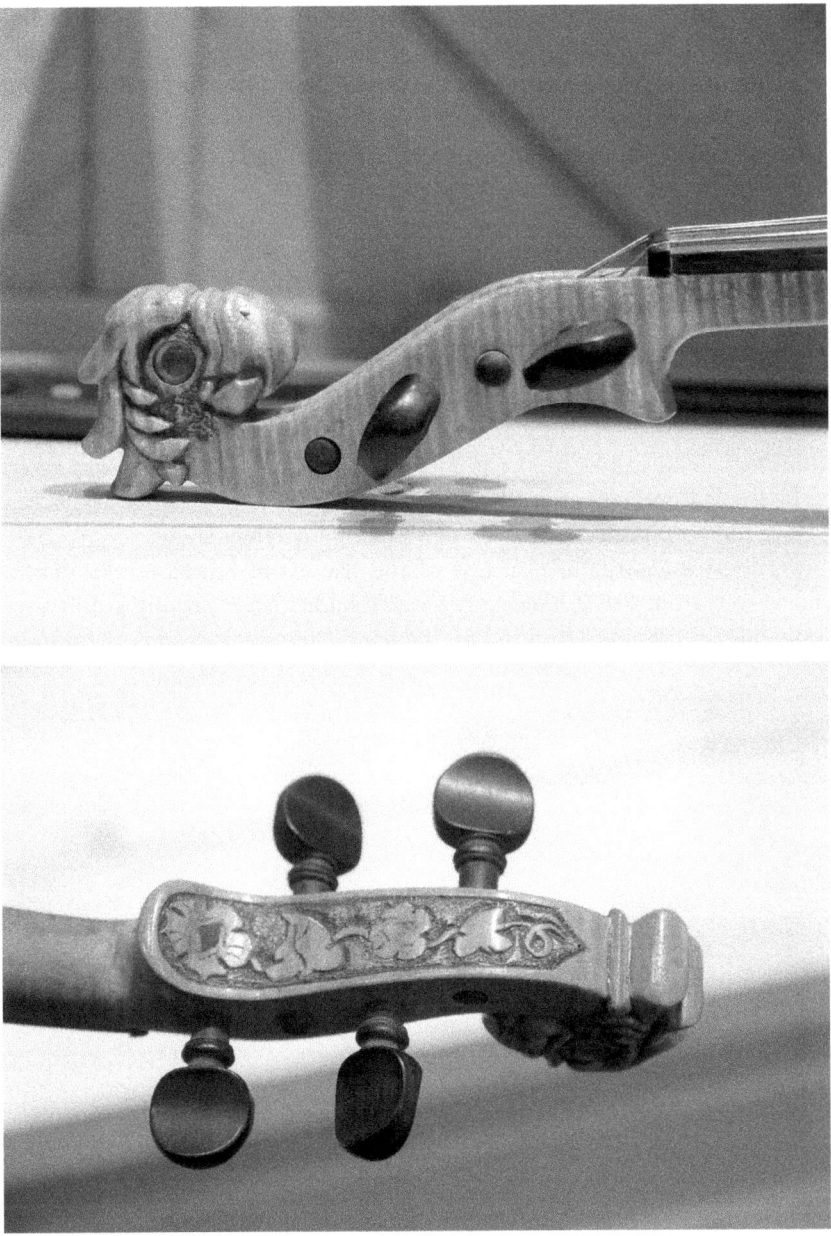

Top: The parrot head carving on one of Albert's fiddles. *Bottom*: Intricate carving on the back of one of Albert's parrot head fiddles (photographs by Jim Kacsmarik).

musician could afford one that cost that much. He regularly sold his fiddles to friends and young people for around $300 apiece, give or take depending on his relationship with the buyer. That price rarely represented the amount of materials, time and loving care that Albert had devoted to creating the instrument, but if someone was going to play it and enjoy it, to Albert, it was worth every minute.

Tuning Up

Albert also managed to win a few fiddle contests in the local area, but he did not play in bands during this time, unless a band needed him to fill in. He was, however, always asked by the Sprague executives to play at company picnics and Christmas parties. One Christmas, Albert was asked to be the featured act after the annual Christmas visit of Santa Claus, but before Albert played there was to be a company talent show.

Albert had organized a few of the friends at Sprague who played music to form a string band. Jerry Smith hadn't been playing guitar very long, but Albert asked him to join the band. He was thrilled at the oppor-

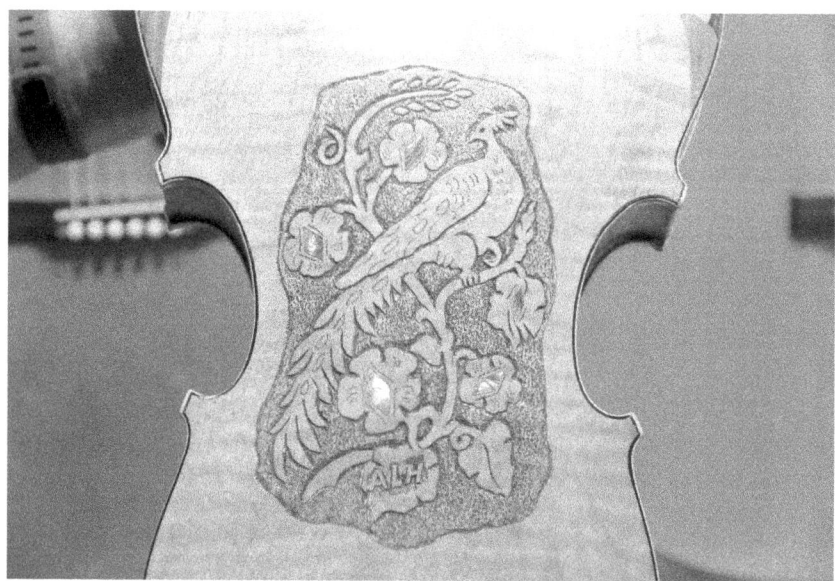

Albert's signature peacock carving on the back of a parrot head fiddle (photograph by Jim Kacsmarik).

Three—Clocks, Machines and "Govn'ment Work"

tunity and spent hours practicing for the big event. When the Christmas party arrived, he was nervous.

Albert, a well-seasoned performer, was used to playing these sorts of gatherings and wasn't nervous about it at all. The other band members, few of whom had performed publically, were a bit worried even though they had spent some hours after work practicing in the machine shop.

The party started at 6 p.m. with the first hour devoted to Santa Claus who gave all of the children of Sprague employees presents and cookies and milk were served. The adult part of the evening was to start at 7:00, and then Albert's band would play in the talent show. At 6:45 Albert dutifully gathered up Jerry and the other band members and said, "Don't you think we ought to go outside and tune ourselves up a bit?"

One of Albert's Sprague Electric bands, ca, 1961. Albert on fiddle, Dean Hart on bass, Jim Poe on the guitar on right, Jerry Smith on left with guitar and unidentified musician (courtesy Kilby Spencer).

Jerry and the band members grabbed their instruments and headed outside with Albert. Albert left one of his two fiddle cases by the door as they headed out. "Aren't you going to need both of those to tune up?" asked Jerry.

"Oh, no, I'll be fine, I just need this one to get tuned up," replied Albert.

When they got outside the school building where the party was being held, Albert ceremoniously gathered the musicians in a circle and said, "OK, boys, let's get ourselves tuned up." He held up his fiddle case, opened it, and, to everyone's surprise, pulled out a slim bottle filled with local white whiskey and preceded to take a drink. The other players quickly set down their instruments and joined him. The machine shop string band then headed back into the building, having "tuned up," and played a set that everyone loved.[9]

Albert's Fiddle Joins the Army

Thornton Spencer, Ethel's brother, continued to come to Albert's house when he could and coax Albert to get his fiddle out and play it so he could learn from Albert's very large repertoire of tunes. In 1960, Thornton enlisted in the U.S. Army and was stationed in Fort Benning, Georgia, and then sent to a remote post in Iceland. With many hours of downtime, Thornton wrote home that he was lost without something to play. Albert, wanting to help, went to work right away and built a fiddle for Thornton. Then he somehow navigated the army postal works, and the fiddle not only got to Thornton, but it also arrived intact. Thornton was thrilled. He whiled away much of his time there entertaining his fellow soldiers and keeping his bowing arm in shape.

Back in the States, when Thornton was transferred back to Georgia, a master sergeant who was trying to organize a band found out that Thornton could play the fiddle and he persuaded Thornton to join. Their first big gig was playing at a very large bar in Columbus. Thornton, two guitar players, an accomplished steel guitar player and an upright bass player took the stage and proceeded to play some of the many tunes Thornton had learned from Albert.

The crowded patrons were heavily imbibing, and the place was jumping. Suddenly in walked the master sergeant accompanied by two new band members, a female singer and a drum player. Thornton and the other

Three—Clocks, Machines and "Govn'ment Work"

band members stood still, perplexed, while the drummer got set up on stage with them and the girl moved a microphone right up in front of the band.

At that point, one of guitar players leaned into the other band members including Thornton and whispered, "Oh no, that drummer can't keep time, and that girl singer, instead of going to a higher pitch, she just gets louder."

Once they got set up, Thornton launched into a fast-paced "Ragtime Annie." It wasn't long before he noticed the drummer not keeping up. The guitar player kept coming over to Thornton to tell him that the drummer couldn't play that fast and they needed to play something else, but Thornton decided to finish the tune. Out of the corner of his eye he noticed that the guitar player had quit playing and was heading toward the back of the stage, toward the drummer.

Suddenly, he heard the drummer holler, "If you don't like it that way, then you can just play it yourself!" Then everything exploded. The drummer and the guitar player locked arms and went rolling off the stage, then stood up in front of the entire audience and started swinging at each other. Then the crowd got into it, bottles and fists flying everywhere. The band, not knowing what to do, just kept playing "Ragtime Annie." Someone had grabbed the microphone from its stand and started swinging the cord overhead like a lariat.

Thornton turned around to see the other guitar player standing next to him with his guitar already packed away. "Get your fiddle in the case," he said. "Let's get out of here. The law is going to be here soon." Thornton and the guitarist headed out the back entrance, jumped into the guitarist's car and headed back to base. The sergeant did not return and they didn't see him for several days because he had landed in jail. That was the definitive end of the military string band at Fort Benning.[10]

A Changing Musical Climate

Back home, early rock and roll had reached even into the mountains, as most homes were now equipped with electricity and at least an electric radio to replace the wind-up Victrola. Elvis and others captured the listeners in the late '50s and '60s, as did the more modern country crooners with electric guitars and drums behind them. Traditional mountain music, at least for the moment, was relatively silent, even in the high Appalachians. With more and more young people driving and more mountain families owning at least a truck, honky-tonk houses that featured electric country music and rock and roll became more accessible.

This had a profound effect on many of the young people of the high mountain hollers and backroads. At a time when they, like Albert and Thornton had done, would generationally be learning the music and old ways of their ancestors in the mountains, some young people were starting to reject their own heritage as "backwards" and "primitive" and were searching for the new lifestyle they heard about on radio and less frequently television broadcasts.

The few times one would hear authentic "old-time" or "mountain" music on radio or television, it was often associated with the stereotypical hillbilly depicted maybe most recognizably by the producers of the popular soft drink Mountain Dew, and to many young people in the mountains this felt degrading. To some, mountain music seemed to represent poverty and ignorance, certainly not brilliance and sanctity as it did for Albert and his friends.

It was in the middle of this cultural chaos that the exact opposite effect was occurring in many cities and suburbs. Some urban and suburban young people were rejecting the new cultural movements brought on by media advertisers and were looking backwards for identity and belonging. They found strength and solace in the music and folkways of the older generations of mountain people. In places like New York City and Boston, Chicago and Philadelphia, "folk" clubs were being formed and young people began to search for recordings of authentic rural music that had been recorded by folklorists both academic and self-proclaimed.

This resurgence, what many people had referred to as "the great folk scare" or the "great folk boom," was causing people to travel the South in search of the "real thing." They were looking for people like Albert, Tommy Jarrell and Fred Cockerham, Doc Watson, Uncle Norm Edmonds, Wade Ward and countless others to counter the complexities of the era with a dose of mountain wisdom.

In 1962, a young fine arts graduate and musician, Art Rosenbaum, came south from New York City looking to record authentic Appalachian music. He had been exposed to the music through friends in the folk clubs in New York and in the newly formed "Friends of Old Time Music" and was enthusiastically pursuing old-time banjo. He wanted

Three—Clocks, Machines and "Govn'ment Work"

to hear and record the music of the mountains in its native state and learn the tunes directly from Southern artists. Rosenbaum brought along a portable reel-to-reel tape recorder and a fiddling friend from Maine.

The two young men had heard that the fiddling convention in Union Grove, North Carolina, would be a good place to hear local music, so they started their journey there. At the festival they fared very well, hearing many local musicians including Uncle Norman Edmunds from Hillsville, Virginia, and they even wound up beating out legendary folklorist Bascom Lamar Lunsford in the band competition. After the convention, the two young men followed a methodology that would one day make Rosenbaum famous: They simply drove from rural town to rural town, asking locals they met who played old-time local music nearby. Then they would follow directions over the winding mountain roads and go meet the musicians, with hopes of recording their music. When they crossed over the state line into Virginia and headed up into the Grayson County highlands, they stopped at a local store and inquired. Everyone in the store enthusiastically told them that they needed to go meet a local fiddler named Albert Hash.

Rosenbaum was surprised to find Albert living in Lansing and working at Sprague Electric, playing local tunes on beautifully crafted, hand-built fiddles. "We were so excited when Albert enthusiastically welcomed us in and agreed to let us record," remembered Art. "His repertoire was large and we realized what a great fiddler he was."[11]

The young men were even more surprised later in the afternoon. Rosenbaum was asking Albert a question about his bowing style when out of the corner of his eye, he saw a small, older woman wearing a shawl peeking out of the kitchen into the living room where the recording session was taking place. It was Albert's mother, Della Mae, up from her usual roost in the back bedroom. "I would like to be recorded, too," she declared to Rosenbaum.

Art was delighted as Della Mae came into the room and sang two ancient ballads into his microphone. He remembered that Alan Lomax had told him that if you were respectful, many people wanted a chance to share their heritage and sometimes their legacies into the microphone. Art can remember that afternoon nearly crystal clear after nearly 60 years.

Albert was gracious and happy to share many fiddle tunes with Art Rosenbaum. He was impressed that Art would travel all the way to Lansing from New York City to record him and he and Ethel showed Art all the hospitality their busy lives could afford. On some of the tracks that Albert recorded, Art Rosenbaum accompanied him on banjo. Della Mae sang unaccompanied. Included in the tracks he recorded of Albert are "Rabbit Up a Gum Stump," "Rose Connelly," "Omie Wise," "Cacklin' Hen," "Soldier's Joy, "Ragtime Annie," "Cricket on the Hearth," "Train 45," "Cluck Old Hen," "Little Log Cabin in the Lane," "Johnson's Old Grey Mule," "Took Her by Her Little Brown Hand," "Flop Eared Mule," "Handsome Molly," "Barbara Allen," "Cumberland Gap," "The Great Physician," "Don't Let Your Deal Go Down," "Cindy," "Black Eyed Susie," "John Henry," "Black Mountain Blues," "Bile Them Cabbage Down," "Who's Calling You Sweetheart Now?," "Tom Dooley," "Darling True Love," "Come All Ye Girls" (ballad by Albert's mother), and "The Dark Haired Girl (ballad by Albert's mother). This array of 28 tunes gives a glimpse of the depth of Albert's repertoire, even in the days when due to family and job responsibilities he was not playing out much. Two of these tracks, "Train 45" and "Omie Wise," were later released on Dust to Digital's compilation "The Art of Field Recording of Art Rosenbaum" in 2007, to great critical acclaim. Rosenbaum would later win a Grammy for the liner notes to this important field recording work.

Heading Back Up Home

After 15 years at Sprague electric, Albert was ready for a change. His fiddle strings had gone slack and it had been a few years since he had built a fiddle. With his girls older now and his youngest, Audrey, begging to learn how to work with wood, Albert and Ethel decided to make some changes. Not only would he leave Sprague, but they would return to the place they both loved and cherished, the Grayson County highlands of Virginia.

Albert bought a small parcel of land on Cabin Creek, right off of the winding, ever-curving Highway 58. He built a modest brick house with a full basement for a shop and plenty of room to host weekly music parties. He also took a new job, in close by Sugar Grove, Virginia. He was going to work for a defense contractor, Brunswick Corporation. The good money it offered would help pay the balance owed on his new house.

Brunswick was a diverse manufacturing company that made a little bit of everything, from bowling shoes to pool tables and records to cabin cruisers. The primary work of the Virginia plant was to manufac-

Three—Clocks, Machines and "Govn'ment Work"

The home Albert built on Cabin Creek off of Highway 58 heading to Whitetop, Virginia (photograph by Jim Kacsmarik).

ture bombs and explosives, but Albert was placed in an area that was a better fit.

Albert's new job suited his skills perfectly. He was a model maker. If Brunswick was going to manufacture something new, Albert would make a model of it first, using wood, plastic or other materials. He was a designer of new products. If Brunswick wanted to build a rocket, Albert would build the hardware, including the casing, and then it would be out of his hands. He did take satisfaction in seeing the finished product.

Though Albert enjoyed his five years at Brunswick, he was glad that he was never asked to participate in their defense projects. Some areas of the plant built explosives—mines and bombs—and Albert sometimes felt bad about the company's mission. "I didn't want to make things to destroy people with," he said, "and fortunately nothing was ever used for that purpose that I made, so I felt a lot better about that. I liked to make it and see it work and then maybe tear it up if it works too good."

Even though Albert considered himself a true mountain man, he didn't like killing of any kind. This philosophy of pacifism echoed throughout Albert's life. "I never wanted to kill the animals, you know," he said, "so

I never hunted or fished. My interest was more in creative work. I'd rather of built the birdhouse than to kill the bird."

"One bird in my life I killed," he continued, "and I killed it by mistake. I was trying to kill a hawk that had been catching the chickens. It was in a tree, and I never could see out any distance like anybody else. So, I shot and this dove fell out of that tree, and I could have cried over it. I didn't want to do that. I never hunted for anything. So, I guess that was one reason they had me working on the instruments and so on, I didn't like to hunt and I didn't want to freeze myself to death out in the woods, so why not cut a pile of shavings on the hearth and sweep them into the fire and come up with a fiddle. Something like that would be worthwhile. Or a dough roller or anything else I took a notion for, if nothing else an ax handle for the ax."[12]

Albert Gets Patented

During his time both at Sprague and Brunswick, Albert created many new machines. Most of them made mundane and rote tasks easier and simpler for the people who did them, and some of them replaced their operators all together. Out of the hundreds of machines he created, including those he built to partially automate his instrument building, he only got a patent on one, and he was forced to do so.

Brunswick management needed a machine that would make tubes by welding Mylar together. They offered the engineers at the plant $5,000 to $6,000 to build one. When Albert heard about it, without thinking twice, he went to work. When his machine, designed strictly in his head and built in his crude machine shop, was finished, he proceeded to make a short piece of tube welded by the heat of the machine he built. He immediately took the tubing he'd built down to the engineering department and asked if "that looked like anything they could use."

Right away, one of the engineers followed Albert back to his two-man shop (Albert had a young apprentice working under him). The machine was sitting in the center of his shop with a tarp over it. The engineer said he came to borrow something, but Albert could tell that he had come to see how Albert had managed to weld the Mylar. He asked to borrow a tool that Albert didn't have and skulked off.

Shortly, the engineer returned to Albert's shop to borrow another tool. He looked all over Albert's shop but Albert once again told him he didn't have what he was looking for. Once again, the engineer took off. On his third trip into the shop, the engineer finally blurted out, "Would you mind telling me how you made that piece of tubing?"

Albert smiled at him and said, "Well, I'll be glad to." He took the tarp off his machine to reveal a small compact unit that looked sophisticated. He plugged it in and waited a few moments for it to heat up. It was made from a simple soldering iron and a wheel Albert had made to roll over the Mylar as it was welded together. It worked beautifully and he began to weld a long length of tube.

The engineer was amazed. He knelt down and carefully examined the machine from all sides. Finally, he said to Albert, "According to science, this thing is not supposed to work." Albert was ready for him and retorted, "According to science, a bumblebee is not supposed to fly, but it does." Then he ran off several pieces of long Mylar tubing.

"And they forgot their machine," Albert said. "They never did anything more to it, but they made me get a patent on that. I didn't want a patent on it, I didn't want any publicity on it or—I didn't ask for any favors," he said. "All I wanted to do was my day's work, you know. That's all I ever cared about. I didn't want any credits for anything."

His superiors told him that he had to have a patent on the machine. When Albert told them he never intended to manufacture the machine, they insisted they needed him to get a patent on it so others couldn't copy it. He told them, "No, I wouldn't fill out a bunch of papers to get a patent on that. I know it's going to run into a bunch of paperwork and that I can't stand—to hear papers rattle!"

However, the Brunswick managers brought the patent papers to him and insisted he fill them out. Once again, he told them he would not fill those papers out.

"They come gathered the papers up and went and filled them out. And they come back and said would you sign this. I signed my name on it. They gave me a dollar for my patent on it." The company then owned the patent but was required to get Albert's permission before they could manufacture the machine. Brunswick never did.[13]

Throughout his 20 years in machine shops, Albert retained his Appalachian philosophy of work and how it should get done. He always believed that an individual could often do more, if left to his own ingenuity, than a department, committee, or work group. This philosophy came from his very upbringing, the way he and his brothers and mother had lived to survive despite of the tremendous challenges poverty and the mountains presented to them. His philosophy was one of raw determinism, solid individualism, and finding one's passion. "One man can work out the details on anything so much better than a dozen can, because they are all looking from a different angle at what you are doing," posited Albert. "And one will see this thing and another will see that thing and they finally agree to disagree on everything and that's what slowed our work down a whole lot. If too many people are involved in something, it begins to drag. I think if you put anything in the hands of a few, you'll come out much better in the long run."[14]

Albert had worked alongside highly educated people at both Sprague and Brunswick and had formed some strong opinions from those experiences. He believed that highly educated people often over-thought projects. He believed that instead of complexity, what was really needed was the simplicity that a hard mountain upbringing had given him.

"And too, I believe, now I'm not downing education in any way, you know, I think it's a wonderful thing," Albert said. "I wish I could've got a lot more of it than what I did. But I think people have studied too much, they think too much, they run way out yonder and they don't see the simpler ways of doing things. They get too complex with doing things sometimes. I think a lot of the things we have in this day and age are that way, so much that they just don't work."

Albert deeply believed in simplicity and originality. He thought the world could and would be a better place if people simplified their daily lives, their jobs and their lifestyles and focused on what they could really do well. "I think a person should keep looking until they find something important to them and that they can be interested in all through their working career," said Albert. "Then it won't hurt you to work. If your work doesn't make you tired, then it won't hurt you, but if you go out to something that you have to do and it makes you tired and you go out there with a bad outlook on life, then that life is going to be short if you keep it up."

Albert also believed strongly that, from what he'd seen, the United States offered too many opportunities for someone to spend his life doing something he didn't like to do. "Our country has too many things to offer, too many fields are open to them. Maybe one would like to be a doctor or a dentist, another a minister, another a blacksmith or machinist or what have you. And they can't swap places. Everyone has his thing in the long run that he would rather do than something else. So I think he'll live longer and be much happier."[15]

Three—Clocks, Machines and "Govn'ment Work"

For Albert, that thing he wanted to do was to build things. And to teach other people how to build things. Things that made mundane work easier, things of beauty and craftsmanship, and things that made beautiful music. After leaving Brunswick and returning to Whitetop, that's exactly what Albert did. He pursued his passions. And that brings us to Eric Clapton's guitar.

Four

Eric Clapton's Guitar

One of the Best

Wayne Henderson is not your typical living legend. He still lives very near his birthplace in Rugby, Virginia, and his daily commute is about 32 steps from his modest home's front door to his daytime (and nighttime) workplace, the Henderson Guitar Shop.

In cluttered disarray of old coffee pots, various machines, and hand tools and pocketknives spread randomly across a variety of wooden workbenches, Wayne conducts his daily business. Here he builds some of the most sought-after musical instruments in the world.

While constantly entertaining a host of visitors that range from neighbors to country and bluegrass music dignitaries, Wayne has managed to build almost 850 guitars in this building. And not just any guitars; Wayne has built some of the best damn acoustic guitars ever made, played by the likes of Doc Watson, Brad Paisley, Norman Blake, Peter Rowan, and, of course, Eric Clapton. A recent eBay sale of one of Wayne's guitars just netted the owner over $18,000. However, none of this, Wayne will be the first to tell you, not one bit of this, would have ever happened to Wayne without Albert Hash. Wayne was also the subject of a recent best-selling book by a reporter from the *New York Times* who embedded himself in Wayne's Rugby shop, waiting for Wayne to build a guitar for Eric Clapton. Clapton, like most other people, waited for years for a Henderson guitar.[1]

Earliest Memory

Wayne's earliest childhood memory, that tiny bit of toddlerhood that cuts through everything in his brain, is of the Hash family. Wayne's father,

Four—Eric Clapton's Guitar

Musician and guitar builder Wayne Henderson (photograph by Jim Kacsmarik, November 2017).

a popular local old-time fiddler from Rugby, had gone to Fees Ridge to visit Albert Hash, probably to get a fiddle bow repaired. Three-year-old Wayne had toddled along. It wasn't an easy trip. Albert's farm was way off the main road and a car or truck couldn't make the last climb up to the house, so Wayne and his dad had to walk the last couple of miles.

When they reached the farmhouse where Albert had his shop, Wayne spied the two Hash girls, Audrey (who was the same age as Wayne), and five-year-old Joyce, out playing in the yard. Wayne remembers heading over to them as his dad was greeted at the door by Albert and Ethel and headed inside. Within a few minutes, Wayne and the girls had wandered straight over to Fees Branch and had waded right in and begun to seriously play in the creek water. Within moments, a screen door banged on the farmhouse and Ethel Hash was standing on the porch, yelling.

Now, one could wager that you could roam to the ends of the earth and not find one other person on the planet who can remember Ethel Hash, the sweet, caring mountain girl, wife to the sensitive and kind Albert Hash, ever yelling at anyone. But Wayne remembers. "I told you girls to never get in that creek by yourselves," she screamed. "And you, Wayne, get out of that water, now!" No one besides Wayne's parents had ever yelled at him and he was so startled he ran into the house to find his dad, crying all the way, scared to death, the moment permanently implanted in his memory. Little did he know that he and the Hash family would become forever linked in history and that Albert would provide Wayne with a lifelong passion for building instruments.[2]

Undated photograph of Albert and Ethel Hash in their kitchen. One of Wayne Henderson's earliest memories is of Ethel scolding him and the Hash girls (photograph by Mark Sanderford).

Four—Eric Clapton's Guitar

The First Henderson Guitar

At the youngest of ages, Wayne became fascinated with the music of one of his neighbors and his dad's close friends, E.C. Ball. Ball had been recorded in 1938 by Alan Lomax at the Galax Old Fiddler's Convention and later in 1941 with his wife Orna on his porch in Rugby. E.C. had also played in a popular string band called the Rugby Gully Jumpers that had included Wayne's father, Walter Henderson, on fiddle. Lomax had also recorded the Gully Jumpers. Alan Lomax had become so admiring of Ball's playing that he had traveled to Rugby in 1941 to capture more of E.C.'s powerful thumb and finger picking mountain style of guitar along with more of the haunting mountain gospel songs that E.C. and Orna sang and played.

Wayne became enamored with the sound of the guitar at age five, and E.C. often let Wayne hold and carefully examine his Martin guitar. Wayne's first attempt to make a guitar involved a snuffbox, a piece of wood for the neck and some fishing line. In fact, he wanted so badly to own his own guitar that at the age of 15, in a manner similar to Albert, Wayne stole to the barn with the flat wood from the bottom of his mom's dresser drawers and tried to fashion a dreadnought. He carefully cut away the outline he had made of E.C.'s Martin guitar and then tried to bend sides to go around, meticulously fashioning a neck from wood lying around the barn.

Wayne found some hoof glue in the barn and tried to put the creation together, but once he tried to put strings on it, it exploded. The glue gave way to the pressure of the strings. Walter Henderson had no idea what his son was up to, but when he came to the barn and found Wayne totally crushed and downhearted by his failed attempt at being a luthier, he knew right away how to remedy the dilemma.

"I know someone who can help you with that," he told Wayne and took him over mountain roads several miles to Albert Hash's new house in Lansing, North Carolina. He had Wayne gather up the pieces of his exploded guitar and bring them to Albert. Albert first took Wayne out to his shop in the old school bus and reached into a drawer and pulled out his favorite fiddle, the Screaming Eagle, and let Wayne hold it.

Wayne nearly came to tears as he ran his fingers over the carefully carved eagle's head on the top of the fiddle. As he turned it over in his hands, he saw the beautiful inlay and carving on the back. He couldn't believe that anyone could single-handedly build anything so beautiful. "Did you really build this, Albert?" he said in awe. Albert proceeded to give Wayne a thorough tour of his shop, showing him how he shaped fiddles, bent the sides and used machines that he had built himself to make the job easier.

Wayne then asked Albert to play that homemade fiddle. When Albert let loose on a couple of tunes, Wayne couldn't believe his ears. It was some of the best fiddling he had ever heard. Wayne, who was playing regularly in a band with his brother, wondered why he hadn't heard Albert playing the local dances. "I've been all tied up with building a house, and work, and family," said Albert, "but I wouldn't mind playing some more now that I'm not going in to work as much."

Albert proceeded to lead Wayne to a little room underneath his house, where he kept some wood. There in the corner was an old mahogany door. Albert picked it up and handed it to Wayne. "You take this and make your sides," Albert said. "This is mahogany, the same stuff that Martin uses in their guitars." Wayne nearly jumped through the ceiling. Then Albert told him how to cut the sides, heat them and shape them in a mold to make gluing the guitar together easier. He took him back to the shop and gave him some wood glue and then loaded him down with a couple of catalogues full of supplies for everything he would need to build a guitar, some proper woodworking glue, and ideas and drawings on paper.

Wayne couldn't believe it. He couldn't wait to get home to the barn to start to work. Over the next several months he ordered a piece of spruce and carefully carved the top and bottom, built heavy braces to ensure that this guitar would stay together, bent the sides in a frame he'd built, and ordered a 4 × 4 × 24" piece of mahogany to carve a beautiful neck to attach to the body. "I braced that thing like a tank," said Wayne. "This one wasn't gonna come apart!" Whenever he could he checked in with Albert and got his advice.

One day about a year after Wayne started his new guitar, his father took him back to Albert's home. Wayne burst into Albert's shop carrying a fully finished, Martin-style guitar. Albert jumped up from his workbench, ran over to take the guitar from young Henderson and exclaimed, "Damn, boy! If I knew you were gonna build something this nice, I would have given you a better piece of wood!" Thus began the legendary career of guitar builder and player Wayne Henderson. It was just the encouragement he needed from someone he deeply admired.

Four—Eric Clapton's Guitar

Albert's First (and Last) Guitar

As Wayne was building that guitar in his barn, Albert decided he, too, would build his first guitar. At that point he had designed and built many fiddles, a couple of mandolins, a few banjos (he loved to experiment with metal, and it is reported that his banjos were loaded with various bits of metal and extremely heavy) but never a guitar. Young Wayne had gotten him interested. In addition, he had a request to build a guitar from a supervisor at Sprague and Albert wanted to please him.

Right away, Albert discovered he couldn't transfer his fiddle building knowledge directly to guitar making. He made the guitar out of beautiful curly maple, like many of his fiddles, and applied his usual detail to the work. Unfortunately, however, Albert had never worked with the thick sides of a guitar and found bending and sizing them to the top and back much more difficult than the thin sides of a fiddle. Wayne, who, by this time, had successfully built and repaired several guitars and had had the opportunity to remove broken tops on a few Martins, was beginning to understand the intricacies of guitar design and construction.

He had offered to help Albert, and one day he came into Albert's shop and noticed that Albert had his entire arm inside the guitar trying to stretch the sides to fit the top. "What in the world are you doing?" he asked Albert.

"Well, let me tell you," said Albert, "if I ever get this thing done, I ain't never makin' another one!"

He had been trying to hold a brace for one of the sides of the guitar in place while it dried. "Anyone who's ever tried to brace something with their hands glued with wood glue knows," Wayne said. "It will take forever and confound you as best it can. It seems like it'll never dry!"

Finally, Albert finished his first guitar and sold it to the plant manager at Sprague. He went to the manager's house to complete the deal, and the manager was thrilled with his new purchase. Albert didn't know this at the time, but it would be the first of many trips he would make to the man's house. The manager had never played a guitar and didn't know where to start; he just knew he liked the sound they made and that Albert was a good builder. He also didn't know how to care for a precious wooden instrument. He took that guitar home and proudly hung it on display in his basement, right above the heat register, for all to see.

After a few weeks, the blowing furnace had heated all the moisture out of the guitar and the beautiful top was full of cracks. He took it back to

Albert and asked him to fix it, and Albert did his best to fill the cracks and refinish the top, but the guitar just disgusted him. A fiddle, having a small body, isn't as affected by heat as a guitar, which has a greater surface area. Not knowing what he was doing to the guitar, the manager kept it over the register and Albert had to periodically reset the neck and fix the cracks in the body caused by the dry heat.

The manager never learned to play, and the guitar hung from a shoestring on a hook in his basement for years. It was still there after both Albert and the plant manager had passed on. In fact, it hung there so long that the shoestring disintegrated. The guitar dropped to the basement floor, hitting the concrete. The bottom end was shattered. There it sat for a few more years.

One day a plumber, a friend of Wayne's, was working on the manager's widow's house, helping her getting it ready for sale. He was going over the plumbing as she was packing things into boxes and throwing things away. While he was outside at his truck, the widow approached him, carrying the guitar. "I don't suppose you'd want this old thing, would you?" she said. The plumber shook his head. "Well, then, I'm just going to throw it out," she declared.

As the woman turned and walked toward the trash bin, the plumber noticed that something was written on the tail block of the guitar. He caught up with her and asked to look at the guitar. There, in full letters, he saw "Albert Hash" clearly written. "Do you want it?" the woman asked.

"No, ma'am," he said, "but I know someone who would want this."

The plumber put it in his truck and drove the guitar straight out to Rugby, to Wayne Henderson's shop. Wayne looked over the guitar, some 40 years after it was built, and recognized it right away. It was his former friend and mentor's only guitar. With loving precision Wayne set to work repairing all of the damage that time, dry air, and the fall off the wall had done to the guitar. It now sits proudly in his guitar collection, in the huge, bank-like vault in his home that guards one of the best guitar assemblages anywhere. In his entire life, Albert never made another guitar. He did, however, repair them many for friends and customers.

"I want to get in there and make some fiddles"

With his years of machining coming to an end after five years at Brunswick and his new home on Cabin Creek nearly finished, Albert began to

Four—Eric Clapton's Guitar

dream about building fiddles again. "I got a pension enough to get by," Albert explained to an interviewer from England. "I have a roof over my head and I don't owe anybody anything. My standard of living is about like that of a pig, but you can get one set too high and you can't make it. If I want to work, I work, and if I don't, I don't. I wanted to get in there and make some fiddles. I didn't want to work until the day I died and get cheated out of all of it."

He built a fine shop in the basement of his new home, with plenty of room for his machines, both store-bought and home-built, and he went about increasing his instrument work. It seemed like his fiddles would fly out the door as soon as he could get them built. He had never numbered his fiddles, but instead had decided to name each one. Many of his fiddles featured corresponding scrollwork or headstocks or beautiful inlay on their backs that corresponded to their whimsical names.

He also decided, at about the same time, to resume his fiddle playing. It was Wayne Henderson who first coaxed him back into the

Top: Front view of the only guitar ever built by Albert Hash. It was restored to its original condition by Wayne Henderson and is now in his collection. *Bottom*: Back view of the only Albert Hash built guitar (photographs by Jim Kacsmarik).

public eye. Wayne asked Albert if he would play with him and his brother and help them put together a band. Albert heard Wayne and his brother Max play and sing at a fiddler's convention in Lansing in the late '50s and was impressed. He thought the boys sounded a lot like the popular Blue Sky Boys. He didn't realize, at first, that it would be their first public appearance, but Albert could see lots of potential in the boys.

The Radio Years

Albert recalled telling himself, "I'm gonna get them boys and I'm gonna have myself a band." He went on to remember, "So I said to them one day, 'Boys, when you have a practice session, I'd like to join you.'" Albert met them in a big empty room where they practiced and could see they had great possibilities, so he joined them.

After a few practices, he suggested to them that they play on the radio. The Henderson boys loved the idea but were terrified.

There was a new AM station in West Jefferson, WKSK, and Albert arranged for the band, the Virginia Carolina Boys, to play live. "So we got ready to go to the radio station, and they just couldn't do it," said Albert. "They were so scared." Albert got an idea. He went to his former bandmate, Jim Poe, who he knew dabbled in sophisticated recording equipment, and asked if he could record the show.

Jim gladly obliged and often joined in, playing and singing with them on what became weekly taping sessions. J.C. Kemp on banjo and, at times, E.C. Ball on guitar often joined them. The recording sessions would often go late into the night: "It would take us until 12 o'clock to make a half hour tape," said Albert. "Somebody would goof up."

Albert, who had played on the radio with earlier bands and often with E.C. Ball and his brother-in-law, Blair Reedy, was frustrated with these recording sessions. He soon tired of them. "'Boys,' I said," Albert remembered, "'there ain't a thing up at that radio station that'll hurt you, just go up there and play it.'" And they did. And the show went over with a bang. They soon had listeners throughout the area and were getting requests to play at schools, dances, and conventions.

For the next eight years, the Virginia Carolina Boys, featuring Albert Hash on fiddle, were one of the most popular bands in the region. They began to pile up requests to play at all kinds of functions. During the years of the radio show, 1966–1974, nearly every significant local musi-

Four—Eric Clapton's Guitar

The Virginia Carolina Boys, including, from left: Albert, Max Henderson, Dick Henderson, Trudy Bell, Boyd Stewart, and country star George Hamilton, IV, preparing to play live on the radio, ca. 1970 (courtesy Carla Osborne).

cian joined them on the air. The lengthy roster included J.C. Kemp, Rector Haire, Jim Brooks, Trudy Bell, E.C. and Orna Ball, Larry Pennington, Vic Daniels, Smith Greer, Bobby Reedy, Fred Cox, Janet Hall, Dean Hart, Ken Powers, Don Stewart, Ken Poe, Hugh Holsby, Rebecca Blevins, Gary Reedy, Raymond Pennington and Otis Campbell.

One of the most frequent guests on the show was Audrey Hash, Albert's daughter. Audrey was particularly popular with fans of the show because she could sing folk songs and mountain ballads like "Barbara Allen," "Rosewood Casket," and "Gypsy Rover" as well as a number of hymns. Always pressed for time on the air, the band would often ask Audrey to leave verses out or shorten the lyrics to the long ballads she chose. This raised the ire of the older listeners and many wrote letters asking for her to sing longer. Albert couldn't have been prouder.[3]

The Wagon Train

The first real live "gig" that the band had was to play at what locals referred to simply as "the wagon train." This was an actual wagon train that traveled from Wilkesboro, North Carolina, in the piedmont region, all the way up the mountain to Jefferson as a special occasion every year. Albert and the band knew, going in, that it was going to be a wild party, as the wagon train had a reputation for getting out of hand.

"You know, every old man that thought they could still be a cowboy would dress up," Wayne recalled. "They would take their guns and shoot and miss. They were dangerous 'cause they all got drunk, that was part of the wagon train. It was the worst drunk scene I've ever, ever played music at." The boys and Albert set up at the Jefferson end and played music for the incoming drunk "cowboys." "It scared me half to death," Wayne recalled. "I'd never been around people who were drunk like that."

The wagon train would stop and camp for a night and set up a full sound stage and have music there. Albert and the Virginia Carolina Boys would sometimes play for the overnight too. "They'd fall off their horses, break their arms and legs, and cause quite a scene," said Wayne. "There's nothing more dangerous than a drunk pretend cowboy who's messin' with a horse!" That was the first paying job that Albert found for the band. He found many more after that—in fact, he often had trouble turning anyone down.

"But if a school needed us, or a church needed us, we were there," recalled Albert. "We drove thousands of miles and spent that many dollars, I guess, going to play for nothing, just for the heck of it." It turns out, almost 50 years later, that it was not for nothing. Wayne Henderson has become, thanks to Albert Hash, not only one of the most revered guitar builders on the planet, but an accomplished entertainer on the guitar who has played Carnegie Hall and the Smithsonian and has traveled Europe and Asia with the "Masters of the Steel String Guitar" tour. Max also developed a reputation as a fine mandolin player and singer before a progressive degenerative brain disease silenced him.

Although Wayne plays many flatpicking tunes that sound much like his dear departed friend and Henderson guitar player Doc Watson, their styles couldn't have been more dissimilar. Doc learned to play not too far away from Rugby, in Deep Gap, North Carolina, but he taught himself to play with a flat pick and helped develop and refine a whole genre of bluegrass and old-time music known as "flatpicking."

It is likely that Albert only met the legendary Doc Watson on one occasion. It was early in his playing career, when Albert was in his 20s or early 30s, and he was playing at a contest near Boone, North Carolina. He remembered to Wayne that the contest was one of the early music contests in which everyone, no matter what instrument they played, was competing against everyone else. The performers were judged on their overall performance, not in instrumental categories like modern-day contests.

Albert recalled that there was a young blind man in the contest who played remarkably on the guitar. Albert won first prize, which at the time was a badly needed sack of flower. However, he thought about that prize long and hard. The guitarist seemed to need that prize just as bad as Albert did. "I thought about giving it to him, but finally decided that I needed it just as badly as he did," Albert told Wayne.

Doc was blind but developed an incredibly acute sense of hearing that allowed him to learn from a variety of sources and transfer notes easily to his flat pick across the strings of the guitar. Wayne, on the other hand, wasn't blind, but was limited by the geography of the mountains he grew up in and his sheltered lifestyle that included daily farm work, chores, school and very little exposure to musical styles other than his neighbors, particularly E.C. Ball. Ball's style involved using a thumb pick rather than a flat pick and then up picking with his fingers on alternate strings to produce a cadence. Wayne not only learned it, but also learned to innovate with the style.

The Man Cabin

As Albert settled into early retirement, he began to seriously develop his basement fiddle-making shop at the house on Cabin Creek. He built several machines to help him in the process of building fiddles. One was a sort of duplicator that had a Dremel tool on one end. Albert could use it to trace the shape of a fiddle back on a piece of wood. He developed specialized sanders and saws that aided in his work. However, he still did much of the carving the way he liked best, holding his trusty razor-sharp pocketknife in his right hand. "I'd just take a piece or two of wood and cut away anything that wasn't a fiddle," Albert said.

After Albert finished the new brick house on Cabin Creek and had moved his mother into the spare bedroom, he decided that Ethel needed her own space, a place to get away and sew and practice the crafts she so enjoyed. Albert decided he would build a log cabin for her, right at the entrance to their drive. So, like every other project, he did some reading, then put down the books and got after it.

For months he carefully sawed timber on the property and carefully mixed a chinking of red clay, mud and water. Slowly, a small beautiful cabin rose up on the property and greeted the many visitors who had started to come visit Albert to hear him play, buy a fiddle, get their instruments repaired in the shop, or to just simply be in Albert's presence. He finished the cabin with handmade shake shingles in the upper eaves and put on a nice tin roof, and then he told Ethel to enjoy it. Ethel moved her sewing machine in and set it up, but it wasn't long until Albert's regular Sunday afternoon jams spilled out of the house and into the cabin. Ultimately it became his "man cave" and Ethel kept her sewing in the house.

A Legend of a Guitar Player

After eight years with Albert, Wayne and his brother, Max, who was a brilliant mandolinist, went on to pursue their own bands and own

The little log cabin Albert built near his Cabin Creek residence. Originally this was going to be a get away for Ethel, but it quickly became a music shack (photograph by Jim Kacsmarik).

Four—Eric Clapton's Guitar

music with Albert's blessing and encouragement. Wayne's path led him to a 30-year recording career, nominations for Grammy awards, and being considered one of the best guitar pickers in the nation. His bands continue to tour nationally and regionally, and he continues to travel thousands of miles to play for churches, schools, and charitable causes and he continues to not make much money playing music.

After playing Carnegie Hall a few years ago, the cab driver who picked Wayne and his fellow musicians up was impressed. "Well, after playing Carnegie Hall, I'll bet you could play just about anywhere you wanted to," the cabbie said.

"Do you think I can still play at the Rugby Fire Department?" retorted Wayne.

Wayne and Albert remained good friends until Albert's death. Over the 25 years they knew each other, Wayne would travel to Albert's shop many times to ask for advice to get out of a particular jam that he encountered working with wood. Sometimes he would travel up the mountain just to get Albert's advice on life. Many times, Wayne would simply sit on Albert's front porch to hear Albert's philosophy of living. He was constantly reminding Wayne that simplicity, kindness and caring in all endeavors, especially those of a human nature, was the mountain way, the way of his ancestors. Although he has become legendary through his guitar building and guitar playing, Wayne has retained the same qualities his dear friend and neighbor possessed. Consequently, he is loved and revered by fans and friends throughout Virginia and the world.

Wayne took a job with the post office and delivered mail throughout the mountains to support his guitar building and playing. In the late afternoon and on into the night, after the mail had been delivered, he built and played guitars in his shop. Much like Albert did with his fiddles, Wayne started each guitar with a carefully selected piece of local wood and built each instrument, as much as he could, with a pocketknife.

One of the things that Albert admired most about Wayne was his wry sense of humor. Humor was another essential for Grayson County mountaineers. It provided both respite from and appreciation for the challenging life the mountains afforded. In order to survive, a true mountaineer had to be able to find humor in the predicaments that living in the mountains put him in, and he had to develop the ability to laugh at himself. Wayne has always been able to do both.

Smedley

During this time, Wayne had come to acquire a huge black commercial turkey that lived at his place. He named the turkey Smedley. Just for amusement, he also took a lot of time helping the turkey develop his somewhat unnatural ability to box. Smedley began to gain a reputation around the county for the boxing exhibitions he would put on with Wayne. Whenever Wayne's name came up in conversation among the locals, someone would invariably ask about Smedley, the boxing turkey.[4]

Often, when the daily crowd that sometimes included Albert and Thornton, came to Wayne's shop in the late afternoon to check on a guitar, get Wayne's advice, pick a tune, or just watch guitars being built, Wayne had a surprise for them. He told them there was going to be a fight that day and they should join him.

He would take his audience outside and there would be Smedley. Wayne would raise his fists and Smedley would raise his wings, and a boxing match would ensue. The two would dance around the yard, taking swipes at each other, gobbling and yelling back and forth while everyone laughed.

Smedley also became famous among the neighbors for running away. Many times, Wayne would be in the shop, building another world-class acoustic guitar, when he would get a call from a neighbor, saying, "Come over here and get this damn turkey!" Smedley would be on the lam, standing on a neighbor's porch.

Wayne could always catch him because once Smedley found a porch, he would see his reflection in the storm door. He just seemed to live to see his reflection in a piece of glass. Once Smedley found a pane of glass, for the next several hours, or however it long it took for Wayne to retrieve him, Smedley would prance back and forth in front of the door, admiring the turkey he could see in the glass.

Wayne would not only have to come get him but would also have to bring a mop and a bucket to clean up the neighbor's porch. Usually by the time he got there the porch would be covered with Smedley's droppings from all that pacing. Wayne would put Smedley in his car, mop the neighbor's porch, apologize profusely and then take his turkey home. Albert loved to tell and collect stories about Smedley and his antics almost as much as he liked for Wayne to tell them.

Over the years since his time with Albert, Wayne has become famous for his unorthodox manner of not ever promoting his guitars and for making some people wait forever to buy a Henderson. It took many years, a trip to the United States from England and a prize-winning reporter's book about Wayne for him to make two guitars for Eric Clapton.

People have tried everything, bribing Wayne with all kinds of things. One customer sent him a dollar a week in the mail for many years (as the mail carrier, Wayne delivered his own mail). Others would show up at his shop on a regular basis and beg. Wayne always decides who he will and won't build a guitar for and when he will build it. The countless letters from all over the world sitting on one of his workbenches are testaments to that. It is rumored that he has orders for well past his expected lifetime.

Getting a Henderson Guitar the Hard Way

One of Albert's dear friends and coworkers, Jerry Smith, who was the engineer at Sprague assigned to write down everything about Albert's inventions, waited patiently for years for a Henderson guitar. He did have one "in" that may have helped: he was the father of one of Wayne's dear

Wayne Henderson checking over one of his hand-built guitars in his Rugby, Virginia, shop, November 2017 (photograph by Jim Kacsmarik).

friends. One day Jerry was working on a high roof on a house and fell off, breaking many bones and nearly dying.

Wracked with guilt, Wayne decided he better finish Jerry's guitar. He told Jerry's family he was going to do it. While Jerry was unconscious, Wayne went to work. Fully recovered, years later Jerry proudly shows his Henderson guitar to visitors. "All I had to do to get this guitar was to fall off a roof and nearly kill myself," said Jerry with a huge smile. "Albert would have loved it."[5]

Wayne finally finished not one but two guitars for Eric Clapton, played Carnegie Hall, has been nominated for a Grammy, has been called the best guitar maker in the world, and still gives all the credit for a lifetime of making and playing the guitar to Albert Hash, who helped him build his first instrument, and E.C. Ball, who showed him how to play it.

Five

The Grooming of a Banjo Player

The Trading Post

Thornton Spencer, Albert's brother-in-law, returned from his stint in the army and came back to Haw Orchard. "He was like a young Elvis," one cousin gushed. "We all, every girl around, had a crush on him." Thornton had kept his guitar and fiddle skills up in the army, playing with various bands on the different posts he served. He was ready to play and the first place he headed was to his brother-in-law Albert Hash's house.[1]

Thornton's family owned a small grocery store on Highway 58, right in the curve near Mt. Rogers School, which he and Albert, and Ethel had attended. Thornton took over as the main proprietor, or at least he purported himself to be. The store had the perfect set-up for the mountains of Virginia. It had scattered shelves filled with canned goods, local herbs, milk, cigarettes and some produce.

There, right in the store's center, was a small woodstove. Thornton quickly arranged several armless wooden chairs around it and began to hold court with his fiddle. Soon a gaggle of musicians came in from the backroads and hollers of Grayson County and Ashe County, North Carolina, and filled the chairs. Albert began to come by almost daily, as did Dean Sturgill, Thornton's cousin, local banjoist Enoch Rutherford, and many other area musicians. In the winter, they'd gather around the stove and play inside the store, and in the summer, they'd play outside in the parking lot or in the shade of the side yard.

Customers soon learned that to buy anything, you just helped yourself and laid cash on the counter by the cash register, because Thornton

Top and bottom: Thornton Spencer, Albert's protégé, in the early 1970s after his return from service, looking like a "young Elvis" (photograph by Mark Sanderford).

was often too engrossed in his fiddle playing to get up and wait on them. Deliveries would come and go and Thornton would often just nod at the deliverymen, pointing with his chin where to leave their wares. Albert and the others often chided Thornton about his clerk skills, but good-natured Thornton just took it in stride. His system seemed to work well, and the store not only survived but under Thornton's direction became also an important musical landmark.

One quandary for the store's customers was the hours of operation. Often Thornton would keep the store open to 11 or midnight so that a good jam could keep going. Depending on the season, he often went raccoon hunting after that. "He mostly wouldn't open that store up until 11 or noon," recalled his cousin, Dean Sturgill. "After the army, I don't reckon Thornton ever saw another sunrise."

The store quickly became a haven for Wayne, Dean, Enoch, E.C. Ball, and many others of Albert's good friends. The warmth of the stove and the promise of a Dr Pepper would lure in many a musician. Word of the ongoing jams spread quickly. The store, originally owned and operated by Thornton's parents, offered him a chance to do two of his favorite things, both of which he thoroughly enjoyed—socializing with his neighbors and other locals and playing music. At the same time, he cared for his two aging parents and helped with their house chores.[2]

Dr Pepper soon became Thornton's favorite drink. When it was first marketed in the mountains, it was said to have healing properties, and Thornton became so fond of the soft drink during his store days he would consume a six pack a day. Today, as he lies buried close to Albert in the small Haw Orchard Cemetery just yards from where Thornton lived for many years, you can find his grave by the six packs of Dr Pepper that family and friends often place there in fond remembrance of a great man.

Coming from Alabama with a Banjo

"It all seems like a dream now," said Flurry Dowe recently from his current home in Southern California. "It was a very strange time, and it just doesn't seem real."

Martin Fox, Flurry's one-time brother-in-law and friend, described it as the "kind of thing that happens to you when you're out all alone early in the morning and you see something special, like a flock of geese, and one of the geese swoops down and honks at you, and there is nobody else to see it. It was one of those moments." They were talking about the time they spent in the Blue Ridge with Albert Hash.[3]

Flurry was 18 years old when he left his Alabama home with his older stepsister in her boyfriend's car. His stepsister, Cindy McLennan, was not much older than Flurry. She and her friend, Martin Fox, a professional photographer, were in search of "authentic" old-time music. They were both somewhat accomplished players but wanted to be around the real thing. Flurry could play one tune on the banjo, "Cripple Creek," but hoped to learn how to really play the instrument in the old-time clawhammer style.

"We picked Flurry up in Montgomery [Alabama] and headed up to Nashville looking for instruments," Martin recalled. "Then it was on to Kingsport [Tennessee]. Then we headed on to Galax [Virginia] hoping to find old-time music. It was around the 4th of July in 1972." After being disappointed by not finding much music, they decided to head back into the mountains and drive south. As they were winding their way up the mountain toward the town of Whitetop, on the ever-twisting Highway 58, they went around a curve and saw a small store, "Spencer's Trading Post," close to a school.[4]

Outside was a very tall man with a moustache and holding a fiddle case. There seemed to be commotion going on both inside and outside the store. All that Flurry, Martin and Cindy could see when they pulled up was a sea of people standing around with the tips of two fiddle bows hitting the air above them. The tall fiddler walked toward them and asked how he might help. Flurry's sister explained they had been looking for old-time mountain fiddle music.

"You should meet my brother-in-law," said the man. He took them into the crowd and introduced them to Albert Hash. Immediately, Martin and Cindy got out their instruments and started to play while locals joined in. The young people couldn't believe their good fortune. They had found what they were looking for. Little did Flurry Dowe know, but he would stay here, as deep in the Blue Ridge Mountains as he could get, and play with Albert and Thornton, two authentic old-time masters, for the next nine years.

After a long while of playing that day Albert stopped, looked directly at 18-year-old Flurry, and asked, "Do you play, youngin'?" Flurry froze. "I just know one tune on the banjo," stuttered Flurry. "Well, let's hear it," said Albert. Flurry nervously played "Cripple Creek" like his sister had showed him. Then Albert asked if he and Thornton could play along. After they

Five—The Grooming of a Banjo Player

played it through a few times, Albert looked at Thornton and said, "I believe the boy is teachable, Thornton." Thornton nodded his agreement and smiled. Thus began the grooming of a banjo player.

Not only did Thornton and Albert welcome the three travelers to the music of the area, they also helped them find a place to live. Martin, who had been a newspaper photographer, was not much accustomed to living in the mountains, so when he was offered a house in nearby Grassy Creek to live in, he jumped at the chance. "All you have to do is help me with my tobacco crop," their new landlord told them.

Martin quickly learned to regret that agreement. Working tobacco was the hardest work he'd ever done.

Banjo Player Training

Over the next several days Cindy and Martin played with locals and got to know Albert while Thornton took Flurry up to a farm to meet old man who played the banjo, Jont Blevins. Jont, whose unique style had made him a local player of some renown, had been overlooked by many of the folklorists who came to the area. Albert, however, considered him one of the best at the older clawhammer style and one of the few players who played the instrument true to the Whitetop Mountain tradition. Jont had learned clawhammer playing as a boy and was taught by Albert's great uncle, Emmett Long, who was born in 1886.

"There is only one man left who can really play the REAL old clawhammer style and that's Jont," Albert told Flurry. He was delighted to meet Jont and the two hit it off right away. In exchange for work around his place, he took Flurry under his wing and began to teach him the Whitetop Mountain repertoire of tunes, and carefully help Flurry learn the unique style of the region. Flurry also began to go over to Thornton's store at least three or four nights a week and play with Albert, Thornton, Dean Sturgill, and other locals. He was becoming immersed in old-time banjo.

Albert was so appreciative that these young people had come from Alabama to learn the mountain music that he introduced them to one of his teachers, Corbett Stamper, who Albert had first heard play on a rainy day as a 10-year-old boy. Martin also began to soak in everything that Albert and the other locals could teach him about fiddling and the music of the Grayson highlands. "But he'd always tell me, 'Don't copy me,'" said

Appalachian Fiddler Albert Hash

The Whitetop Mountain Band in the Spencers' store, ca. 1976. From left, Albert Hash, Emily Spencer, Flurry Dowe, and Thornton Spencer (photograph by Mark Sanderford).

Martin. "You don't want to play like me. Get that fiddle up under your chin so you can play all kinds of music."

Flurry took to his total immersion in mountain music very quickly. Before six months was up, Thornton and Albert were taking him with them when they played schoolhouses and dances in the area. Flurry would play the banjo while Albert fiddled and Thornton played guitar, or if a guitar player came along, Thornton would accompany Albert on a second fiddle. "He played more banjo in those first six months than most people play in a lifetime!" Thornton recalled.[5]

Flurry would also visit Jont regularly, and Martin often went along to soak up everything that Jont could teach him about living and playing in the mountains. "He was way back up this mountain road," recalled Martin, "and it was like stepping back a century. Jont lived in this little house with no running water and no electricity and was self-sufficient. He taught us a lot about how to live in the mountains besides teaching us about music and turning Flurry into a banjo player."

Albert and Thornton began considering Flurry's visits with Jont and their nightly sessions at the store or weekend jams at Albert's house as his "training" to be their banjo player. "I think they chose him because he didn't know enough yet to have a style of playing," Martin said. "They were molding him to be their banjo player. They knew Jont would teach him how to play in the local style, and that's what Albert and Thornton did best, is play in the local style." Albert came to love the way Flurry had learned the mountain style so much that he told one interviewer, "He's only 20 years old, but he's been playing for 75 years."[6] The Flurry Dowe experiment seemed to be a success.

Learning the Whitetop Ways

Albert and Thornton also enjoyed the way Martin played the fiddle and Cindy played the guitar and they were spending every weekend playing at Albert's house or at Thornton's store. Martin considered them surrogate parents to him, Cindy and Flurry; they felt adopted and loved. And soon, like parents, Albert and Ethel began to make strong overtures toward Martin and Cindy that they ought to get married. Cindy and Martin succumbed to the pressure and got married, with Albert and Ethel Hash serving as their best man and bridesmaid.

In the meantime, Thornton wasn't above putting them to work. In the fall his aging parents, who Thornton lived with while minding their store, needed wood for their winter heat. Thornton's mother was worried because her husband had had a stroke and had "gone simple," as the older mountain folks, like Mrs. Spencer, said. The stroke had left him unable to perform daily chores. Thornton had a reputation locally for avoiding any kind of hard work that did not involve a fiddle and a bow and so he seized the opportunity to enlist Martin's help.

Thornton approached him delicately and explained his parents' dire predicament, telling Martin how bad the winter could be if his parents didn't get some much-needed firewood and that he "had many other important things to do." He also just happened to know of a dead apple tree that needed to be cut down near the Spencers' house.

Martin was convinced. He borrowed a chainsaw from a neighbor and went to work while Thornton headed off to the store to play fiddle, drink his daily six-pack of Dr Pepper, and conduct business around the woodstove. Martin toiled most of the day cutting and carefully stacking cords of wood on the Spencers' porch. At the end of the afternoon, Thornton came back to his parents' house to see the progress that Martin had made. He admired the wood that was stacked and he also admired the fine dinner his mother had spread out on the table: two chickens she had killed and fried while the wood was cut, mashed potatoes, gravy, green beans and all the fixings.

As Thornton sat down in his usual chair at his mother's table, she told him, "Get up and let Martin sit down!" When Thornton asked why, she

Undated photograph of the Spencer family. From left, Ethel Ruth Spencer (Hash), Audrey Wave Spencer, Thornton Spencer, Zollie Mae Spencer (Owen), and Orie Lance Spencer (courtesy Carla Osborne).

told him, "'Cause he's the only one who does any work around here." Martin enjoyed his supper a great deal while Thornton just looked on from the other room. "It made that meal taste even better," said Martin.

Albert's Unfailing Kindness

When you ask someone who personally knew Albert what his or her first memory of Albert is, the first thing you generally hear is that he was one of the kindest people that he or she ever knew. Flurry, Martin and Cindy learned a lot from spending so much time with Albert Hash. One of the traits they noticed that Albert and many of his neighbors possessed was a natural disposition that favored kindness and caring. Sometimes Martin felt that they had stretched their welcome to the maximum, taking advantage of all the gifts of music, food, friendship and teaching that Albert, Thornton, and the others could give.

One example of Albert's kindness came when Flurry's older brother paid a visit from Montgomery. Having not lived in the mountains and full of city life, the brother stood out among the locals nearly everywhere they went. His extremely long hair and attitude often attracted a lot of looks from the locals. One night at the Grayson County Fiddler's Convention (held at that time in the ballpark in Independence, Virginia), Martin, Flurry and the brother were sitting in the bleachers listening to the contests on stage when the brother declared, "I'm gonna get high."

He had been eyeing some woods attached to the ballpark and decided he would head over to them to smoke some marijuana. In the 1970s, in the rural South, this was a very bold move, to say the least. Martin tried his best to dissuade his brother-in-law, pointing out the many local sheriff's deputies that were patrolling the park. Flurry's brother could not be deterred and headed for the woods behind the ball field.

Sure enough, a few minutes later, Martin and Flurry watched as the brother was surrounded by officers and thrown into a patrol car and taken to jail. The young men didn't quite know what to do, but they knew who to ask for help. When Albert finished performing in the contest with Thornton and a band, they hesitantly approached him and let him know what was happening. They weren't at all sure how Albert would respond.

Albert listened quietly to their story, turned to Thornton and asked him for the money they had just won in the band contest. He told Flurry to get in the truck with him and drove to the county jail. There he took the contest winnings and put up the bail for Flurry's brother so the two could spend the rest of his brother's visit together. Nothing else was said of the mishap. Martin never forgot the kindness Albert showed, without flinching a bit, that day.

Albert Rededicates His Life to Music

After seven years playing on the radio with the Henderson brothers, and now fully retired from machine work, Albert had decided that he wanted to spend more time concentrating on fiddle building and playing the old-time music that he had grown up with.[7] Wayne Henderson and his brother Max had drifted to playing more bluegrass-style music, as the style of Wayne's friend Doc Watson and other guitarists was becoming more popular and an integral part of the bluegrass sound. The popular run of The Virginia Carolina boys had made Wayne quite well known in

Albert playing a tune for Ethel on their Cabin Creek porch, 1975 (photograph by Mark Sanderford).

guitar circles and had gotten Albert back out performing and competing in contests and conventions across the region.

Both he and his beautiful fiddles were getting lots of attention, especially among the younger people who were discovering old-time music across the country. Consequently, his new home on Cabin Creek was beginning to receive a steady stream of visitors from across the country that wanted to purchase a fiddle, play a tune with Albert, or to learn from him about the music of the area.

Albert consciously decided that he really wanted to focus the rest of his life on two things: one was preserving the local music, the original old-time music he had learned as a teenager, and two was to build fiddles to bring joy to others and to teach others to build fiddles and play the music. So the two intricately linked instrument builders of Grayson County, Wayne Henderson and Albert Hash, each turned to their favorite music and to their respective shops and created separate legacies, only separated geographically by a few mountain miles.

Wayne, Albert and Max remained great friends and Albert would often ask Wayne to back him up in fiddle contests throughout the region, contests that Albert usually won. Wayne continued to visit Albert's shop on a regular basis and Thornton, Martin, Flurry, Cindy and their friends were regular guests at Wayne's guitar shop in Rugby. One of the great joys of a visit to the Rugby shop was that you never knew what you would find going on there. It could be a lesson in guitar building, a world-class jam session, or even a boxing match involving a turkey.

Rounder Recordings

In the early 1970s, a young folklorist and banjoist named Blanton Owen and his friend Tom Carter came to the area to record local musicians. The National Endowment for the Humanities funded the recording trip. Owen and Carter, at the time, were also members of the Fuzzy Mountain String Band, a popular revivalist string band. Owen played banjo while Carter played mandolin and guitar. They had just released an album on the newly formed Rounder Records to some acclaim among folk enthusiasts. The folklorists had been travelling throughout southern Virginia, in Grayson, Carroll, Patrick, Franklin and Floyd counties, collecting fiddle and banjo playing as part of the NEH project.

They recorded several local musicians in Albert's area including

Jont Blevins, banjoist Stuart Carrico from around Independence, Virginia, and Albert's neighbor, Corbett Stamper, as well as Albert and Thornton Spencer, among many others. Albert, who was gaining popularity from his performances, contests and fiddle making, was used to people coming to Whitetop to record him and so did not consider these sessions out of the ordinary. Apparently, he just figured the two young men wanted to learn some new tunes and to study his playing style, so he gladly obliged.

Owen and Carter, after finishing the project, believed that the breadth and depth of the recordings they'd made across southwest Virginia were worthy of a wider audience and began to negotiate for a record label. In 1976, Rounder Records released a two-volume set of some of the recordings called *Old Originals*. Albert is featured on two of the tracks: a Whitetop version of "Cripple Creek" played with Paul Spencer on banjo and Jones Baldwin on guitar and "Nancy Blevins" with Thornton backing him on guitar.

When the album was released, Albert was not happy. Owen had not talked to him about the album release, and he felt that he and the other musicians didn't approach the recordings knowing that they would eventually become commercially available. "He didn't tell us what he was doing, you know," Albert said about the recordings, "and nobody cared if they played good or bad. I was ashamed of it. If he'd have told people it was for an album, they'd have played much better, you know."[8]

Albert, who was an advocate for the local music and musicians, felt like Owen and Rounder Records had duped him and the others. "He didn't care, you know," Albert said. "They [Rounder] didn't want it to sound good. They thought these local musicians was supposed to be rough and sound bad and that's the worst mistake they ever made in their life. There's some of them fellows that can really play it, you know, and they don't play rough. They play a lot of the old tunes that the colonists had when they come over here."[9]

Thornton Finds a Match

In 1975, a young woman came to the Whitetop area to study music and the local culture. Her name was Emily Paxton, and she was a student at the Clinch Valley College of the University of Virginia. She was from a well-heeled Arlington, Virginia, family but loved old-time music and

Five—The Grooming of a Banjo Player

those who played it. She was also an accomplished singer who loved to sing the old-style ballads and played guitar, fiddle and a bit of banjo.

Her course of study at Clinch Valley College was social welfare and sociology in a department that was under the direction of Dr. Helen Lewis, a well-known advocate for Appalachian women and a firebrand who believed deeply in the integrity of the culture of Appalachian residents. She had encouraged Emily to pursue her interests in Appalachian music, and in the summer she was finishing her degree, Emily traveled to Grayson County to study the unique sound of the Virginia's highest mountains. Almost right away, she fell in love with the music and the people who lived in the area.

On her first trip to Grayson, she met up with a girlfriend and they decided to go seeking music. They stopped in at Thornton Spencer's store and there she heard Corbett Stamper and was in awe. Her friend, Susan Cahill, suggested that they head down to Independence to a fiddle festival happening there. Susan's friends Flurry Dowe, Martin and Cindy Fox decided to join them.

After enjoying the festival, they heard about a party at Stuart Carrico's house. He was a banjo player in his 70s who had been recorded by

Emily Paxton Spencer and her husband, Thornton Spencer, shortly after their marriage in August of 1976 (photograph by Mark Sanderford).

Owen Blanton so they knew there would be good music there. He lived just down the road from the festival and they headed that way.

When they arrived, there on the steps of Carrico's house was Thornton Spencer, playing the fiddle. Immediately, Emily was deeply attracted to the handsome, soft-spoken and talented man and secretly asked her friends if he was married. When she found out that he wasn't, she sidled right over to him and began a conversation. Even though Thornton was almost 17 years her senior, he was intrigued by this bright, beautiful and outspoken young woman. He, too, was attending college at the time, using the GI Bill to study at Wilkes Community College.[10]

After a lot of talking, he invited her out, and they seemed to hit it off. She and Thornton began to travel together to area festivals and parties, sprouting a romance that would endure the next 41 years. Soon Emily was a regular fixture at Spencer's Trading Post, playing with Albert, Flurry, and whoever else stopped by. When Emily played guitar, Thornton was freed up to play twin fiddles with Albert.

The two brothers-in-law loved to play together, and they created a unique twin fiddle sound. In August, Emily graduated from Clinch Valley College and decided to stay in Grayson County. Soon, she and Thornton, Flurry and others formed a band to compete in contests and play local dances.

Albert's Style of Fiddling

"I don't know anything about music," Albert once told a fiddling class at the Augusta Heritage Center in Elkins, West Virginia. "All I know is the homemade notes."

Albert knew enough to play in several fiddle tunings besides standard tuning. He played many tunes in EAEA, or "cross tuning," as many fiddlers call it.

"The older timers around me had about five different ways they tuned these things," Albert recalled, "so that certain strings would drone." Albert would use each of these tunings, some for just one or two melodies he knew. "There was also 'High Bass' tuning, that I use quite a bit. There is another one for 'Black Mountain Blues' and so on," Albert said.

He would often take two or more of his homemade fiddles with him to shows, each tuned in a different tuning, so that he wouldn't have to re-tune onstage. The style he played was a mixture of influences, both those

Five—The Grooming of a Banjo Player

Albert, ca. 1975, doing what he loved: jamming with other musicians (photograph by Mark Sanderford).

of the older fiddlers around him like his great uncle George from whom he learned much of his reputation. Albert was also a careful listener, and he also had collected licks from Arthur Smith, Lowe Stokes, G.B. Grayson, and others that were in his record collection.

"He had a clear, notey style," recalled musician and music historian Paul Brown, who knew Albert. "It was old-time fiddle style, but it was distinctive. He followed melody very carefully in ways that some other fiddlers did not."

Brown placed his playing style as distinct to his region. "He was somewhere, for me, between the old Galax-style fiddlers like Luther Davis and Emmett Lundy, and the bluegrass style, and people like Uncle Norm Edmonds and Tommy Jarrell, who were very rhythmic and very percussive and syncopated in their style. He was somewhere in the middle. You could hear a bit of the influence of Arthur Smith, and the influence of older Grayson County fiddlers. His fiddle playing was faster and had a sharpness that I appreciated."

Paul Brown summed up Albert's fiddle playing by saying, "In the end, he was Albert. He put his own signature on every tune he played. You knew where he was from and who he was. That style, the Whitetop style, has not gotten as much attention as some other styles of fiddling, but I think it should. People should listen to it and learn it."

Musician Brian Grim prides himself on being one of the few people who really captured Albert's bowing style. "He called it circular bowing," said Brian, "because your right arm is always in motion. Therefore, there is much power in it, like winding up a clock. It took me a long time to learn it, but once I did, it helped my playing a lot."

"His was a powerful style," recalled musician and luthier Joe Thrift. "It's sad to me that Albert never really got the recognition for his playing that Tommy Jarrell did, because Albert was every bit as good a fiddler as Tommy, in his own way. Those of us who got to listen to him knew it."

Albert's Reputation Grows

Albert was back into music nearly full-time when he wasn't in his shop building fiddles. He would grab local guitarists as well as banjo players and fiddlers and enter or perform at all of the many local festivals in Grayson and surrounding counties. Through word of mouth, his fiddles were beginning to be seen far and wide, and young people from across the nation flocked to his shop to order a fiddle or to attend a Sunday jam at the Whitetop fiddler's home on Cabin Creek.

Young people from New York City, California, Minnesota, Wisconsin, and even Ireland were traveling to Albert's Cabin Creek home to hear him play and to examine the many fiddles he had built and others that he collected and repaired. Winning more than 50 ribbons at various conventions and contests had boosted Albert's reputation to a national level among the folk revivalists. Among the young people who started regularly visiting him were singer and musician Alice Gerrard, Wayne Erbsen, Mac and Jenny Traynham, Paul Brown, Andy Cahan, Field Recorders Collective founder Ray Alden, a young John McCutcheon, David Holt and many others, a virtual "who's who" of old-time and folk musicians.

Each and every one of these visitors was overwhelmed by Albert's generosity and kindness in sharing skills in instrument building and in teaching fiddle tunes and returned often to visit him. Starting in about 1975, one of those newcomers was a 20-year-old John McCutcheon, who had

Five—The Grooming of a Banjo Player

An advertisement for the 1978 Saltville Old Time Fiddler's and Bluegrass Convention featuring Albert Hash (courtesy of Martin Fox).

talked his University of Wisconsin music professors into a three-month independent study in Appalachian music.

"That three-month course has gone on for well over 40 years now," said John. "It just took over my life." John was learning to play banjo, fiddle, mountain dulcimer, hammered dulcimer and virtually any instrument with strings. He was drawn to Albert's powerful but crystal-clear approach to the old mountain fiddle tunes and was deeply moved by Albert's kindness and encouragement.[11]

Working with a group of organizers in southern Virginia and Kentucky, John helped found and solidify Appalshop, a mountain collective that would eventually put down roots in Whitesburg, Kentucky, and become a driving force for mountain music as well as the very welfare of the Appalachian culture and its people. Albert's intense appreciation of the people of his area and for the tradition of the mountains deeply influenced John's life and his work as a musician and an advocate over the next 45 years.

Martin and Cindy, who had by now moved out of the high country, were regularly playing a particular fiddle tune that they had learned from Albert called "Hangman's Reel." They were spreading the tune in jams across the region and teaching Albert's version of it. The tune had also begun to appear in recordings made of Albert in about 1973 and quickly became a part of his regular performance repertoire. It was an unusual tune with four parts that built melodically to a great crescendo and anyone who heard Albert, Thornton, Martin, or Cindy play it wanted to learn it right away. Soon, the tune found its way to nearly every fiddling convention in the United States. Almost always, the tune is associated with Albert Hash.

"Hangman's Reel"

In reality, "Hangman's Reel" was a Canadian tune that Albert had learned from a record of a Texas fiddler, Bill Northcutt. Many folklorists believe the tune may have derived from a Canadian traditional tune called "Reel du Pendu" ("Hanged Man's Reel"). In any event, Albert made the tune his own and what he played and recorded did not closely resemble either Northcutt's or the Canadian version. Albert also learned another tune from Northcutt that became a Whitetop Mountain standard, "Old Sport."[12]

Sometimes Albert would introduce the tune with the legend that still often accompanies it at performances by old-time musicians or in jams. The most common Southern version of the story is that a man "way up there in Canada" was headed for the gallows on the day before the tune's creation. The man was locked away in a cell for a dastardly crime that

Five—The Grooming of a Banjo Player

had nearly been forgotten. Outside his jail cell window, he could hear the gallows being built, nail by nail. The prison was well constructed, and although he wanted badly to escape, he couldn't find a way out.

As he looked through the bars of the cell inside the jailhouse, he noticed an old weathered fiddle and a bow on the wall. An idea came to him right away. He immediately called the jailer over and told him that he was the greatest fiddler the jailer had ever heard, and if the jailer would only let the prisoner play, he would prove it. The shrewd jailer, of course, after questioning the prisoner about fiddles and fiddling, didn't believe that this lowly man was a renowned fiddler. A great argument ensued, and after several minutes of arguing and yelling, the prisoner convinced the jailer to make a bet with him.

The prisoner got the jailer to bet that he would be set free if he could prove that he was a great, accomplished fiddler. The prisoner agreed that if he was lying about his fiddling ability he would go quietly, without incident, to the gallows the next day. After they shook hands on the bet, the jailer allowed the prisoner to have the fiddle and bow from the wall and keep it overnight. With the noose around his neck and standing on the gallows over the trap door, he would get his chance to play the fiddle the very next day.

The problem was that the braggart inmate had never played a fiddle in his life. It was the only idea he had come up with to try to save his own life. He nervously grabbed the bow and stayed up all night long, dragging the bow across the strings, hoping a tune would emerge. The next morning, when the jailer came to take him to the gallows he was shaking and covered with sweat. As they approached the gallows, the prisoner began to cry and pray for forgiveness. As the noose was put around his neck, the jailer stared at him, as did the crowd that had gathered for the hanging.

Slowly, the doomed man raised the fiddle to his chest and raised the bow into the air. As the bow struck the strings, a tune emerged that soon had the crowd dancing. He had named the tune "The Hangman's Reel."[13] In most versions of the story we never get to know if the fiddler lived or was hanged. There are many variations on this story; in some he is given the fiddle for the first time on the gallows, and in others he is instructed to play "Hangman's Reel" or the "Hanged Man's Reel" to win his freedom.

In 1984, a year after Albert's death, John McCutcheon, who by that time had become an international star and recording artist, was asked to perform at a large folk festival just outside of Milan, Italy. As John carried his load of instruments toward the large stage assembled on the festival grounds, he heard a group of young Italian musicians having a raucous jam session in one corner of the park. When John approached them, he recognized the tune they were enthusiastically playing. It was Albert Hash's version of "Hangman's Reel" played just as he had recorded it with the Whitetop Mountain Band. John nearly cried as he listened and thought immediately about calling Albert to tell him, and then remembered that Albert was no longer alive in his beloved mountains.

"Nancy Blevins"

Another tune that Albert often played in contests and performances and at dances was much sought after by his many fans and students and began to make the national circuit of old-time music jams. This tune, "Nancy Blevins," was one of Albert's favorites from early in his playing and had close historical and familial ties to Albert himself. It seems that the fiddle tune "Nancy Blevins" was written by a relative of Albert's named, of course, Nancy Blevins. From all accounts Nancy was a fine fiddler and performed in the local area at house parties and dances when Albert's grandfather was a boy, just after the Civil War.

According to the story Albert often told, Nancy Blevins was his grandfather's cousin. Albert's grandfather had told him about her and her fiddling and had said that he had "danced to 'Nancy Blevins' just after the Civil War when he was two years old, wearin' a dress like little boys used to wear in those days."[14] Albert himself had learned the tune from Jim Reedy, who had learned it from his father, Bob Reedy.

Albert said that his grandfather, Benjamin Hash, could remember one verse of the tune that went "I've played this fiddle till it cramps my hand, nary another tune till I get another dram." Albert had been told that the tune had originated in Crumpler, North Carolina, in Ashe County, a considerable distance over mountainous terrain from Grayson County where Nancy Blevins had lived and his relatives had settled.

Historian Josh Beckworth, in his definitive history of Grayson and Whitter, spent considerable time trying to unravel the origins of the tune "Nancy Blevins."[15] After comprehensive research, Beckworth found no blood relation between the Blevins family in Ashe County and Albert's grandfather's family as Albert often claimed. He did find, however, that Nancy Blevins did exist, was a successful young fiddler right after the Civil

War, and continued to play most of her life, eventually marrying and becoming Nancy Baker.

It turns out that not only did Nancy Blevins play fiddle, but, according to Beckworth, was reported to be a mountain witch, who was familiar with the use of herbal medicine and spells. She also had lived for quite some time in a house that was, ironically, right next door to the house that Henry Whitter would later live in, the very house where Albert would often stay as a teenager when he went on the road playing with the great songster.

Incredibly, Albert had brought forth a tune that was native to the mountains near his home that his grandfather had danced to and that was played by a witch who lived in a neighborhood that he frequented as a young man. That very thread of circumstances surrounding the tune is so indicative of the folk process that Albert loved. Thanks to Albert's recordings and persistence in telling and retelling stories about the woman who wrote it, "Nancy Blevins" lives on in jam and recording sessions across the world.

"The last leaf on the tree"

As more and more young tune collectors flocked to Grayson County and the surrounding area to visit the "old-timers" like Albert, Tommy Jarrell and Fred Cockerham in nearby Surry County, North Carolina, Wade Ward in Galax, Uncle Norm Edmonds in Hillsville and many other local Blue Ridge musicians, Albert felt pressure. He became worried that he couldn't teach them well enough in the short amount of time he had with them. He wanted to make sure that they had a chance to learn the music he so loved, the music of the high mountains of Grayson County. Albert described his frustration:

> Lots and lots of young people about that time, more so than now, was travelling the roads with a little banjo on their shoulder or a fiddle in a wooden case and they was doing their utmost to learn this old time old traditional mountain fiddling. And they had a poor chance of learning it because I'm almost the last leaf on the tree when it comes to that.
>
> Now there's a difference in our music up here and that down around Galax. They have what we call the Galax sound. Ours goes on back from, say, Independence back through Abingdon, Bristol, over into Tennessee, up into Kentucky and round about. This is entirely different down this way. They are wanting to learn that.[16]

Albert truly saw himself as "almost the last leaf on the tree" for a wide swath of old-time music in his area. He used that phrase many times over the years when friends, students and family would query him about his dedication to teaching and sharing old-time music. For that very reason, at the age of 54, he decided to record his first album of fiddle tunes. He went to Galax and looked up an old friend, a banjo player and fiddler named Kyle Creed, and told him, "I want you to record some of my old fiddle tunes. These young fiddlers want to learn it and they can't learn it around these fiddlers' conventions and places like that. They get all confused and just half play it and then they go off and they think they can play it." Albert was worried about the legacy of Whitetop music and so he decided to lay it down on vinyl the best he could.

Mountain Records

In early 1976, Albert gathered a group of musicians to play on the record he hoped would capture the Whitetop area sound. He called the band The Whitetop Mountain Boys, even though Thornton's new wife, Emily, was prominently featured on many of the tracks. It was decided that each side of the LP would feature a different fiddler so that Thornton could demonstrate his fiddle ability and some of the tunes he loved to play on one side and Albert could play his favorites on the other.

There were really two bands on the album; side one featured Albert on fiddle, Flurry Dowe on banjo, and Thornton on guitar, and side two featured the configuration of Thornton on fiddle, Flurry on banjo and Emily on guitar and vocals. Emily's singing figured heavily on side two, while side one was all instrumental. Both sides had six cuts.

Kyle Creed, the producer, was a much-loved musician who fronted a band called the Camp Creek Boys and often played with local North Carolina legends Tommy Jarrell and Fred Cockerham. Kyle, like Albert, was a musician and a luthier. He had learned to play the banjo at age 15. As had Albert, he had made his first instrument himself and had been building them ever since. Kyle was a carpenter by trade, but spent every spare minute playing music or building banjos.

In the mid–1960s Kyle had been recorded on several banjo anthologies and decided that he was ready to do his own recording. He put his carpentry skills to work and helped his business partner on the venture, musician Bobby Patterson, build a recording studio near Bobby's home.

Five—The Grooming of a Banjo Player

The two set to work on some of the seminal old-time and early bluegrass recordings of the time. While Bobby built the studio, they split the cost of recording equipment and supplies. They called the venture Mountain Records and their 1972 debut album was *Blue Ridge Style Square Dance* featuring Kyle, Bobby, and the Camp Creek Boys. The label's second release, also in 1972, became legendary. Entitled *June Apple: Old Time Fiddling and Clawhammer Banjo*, it featured Tommy Jarrell on fiddle and Kyle on banjo with Bobby Patterson playing bass.[17]

Those two releases put Mountain Records squarely in the bins of nearly every folk and country record store in the nation. Kyle soon followed with more releases of his playing, including *Mountain Ballads* and his very popular *Liberty* album as well as records featuring other bands such as the Pine River Boys from Carroll County, Virginia.

In 1976, impressed with Kyle's work, Albert gathered his friends and family and recorded the album *Whitetop*. It was Mountain Records' eleventh release and it served two purposes for Albert: one, to have something to give to students who trekked to his house to learn the Whitetop sound, and two, as a chance to preserve some of his and Thornton's playing.

Kyle was the primary producer on the first Whitetop album and he had a reputation for being a bit cantankerous to work with. He recorded part of the album in Albert's living room on Cabin Creek and would run through the house, demanding that heaters be shut down and activity in the kitchen stop for the recording session. The resulting tracks have a very "down home" quality to them that Albert wanted. Interestingly, Albert chose some local tunes and some not-so-local tunes to play on his debut recording. He chose the tunes that he most liked playing at the time from his repertoire of 80 or more tunes.

They included both "Hangman's Reel" and "Old Sport," learned from Texas fiddler Bill Northcutt but played in Albert's Whitetop style; "Rabbit Up a Gum Stump," a tune associated with Hiter Colvin, a Louisiana-born fiddler; "Lost John," a tune that served as a tribute to Henry Whitter who had recorded it on the harmonica and from whom Albert had learned it as a teen; and "Little Brown Hand," one of Albert's favorites, that he had learned from Tennessee fiddler Arthur Smith.

The cover of the album features a photo of Albert, Thornton, Emily and Flurry gathered around the woodstove in Spencer's Trading Post. Thornton, of course, is drinking a Dr Pepper and smoking a cigarette, a look that would characterize his next 40 years of playing with the Whitetop Mountain Band, both onstage and off. Albert radiates with a welcoming smile and the look of pride of an accomplished musician.

Thornton, although he loved to play his own style of Whitetop fiddle, had become one of Albert's biggest supporters and promoters. He was always telling folks about Albert's fiddles and the skill with which Albert played the fiddle. As the Whitetop Mountain Boys began to become a performance and contest band, Thornton often had to take the place of second fiddle to Albert's on-stage hijinks, which by now included some trick fiddling, including playing "Arkansas Traveler" behind his back with the fiddle upside down.

Thornton seemed to enjoy playing second to Albert but was also often featured in a segment of their performance highlighting his unique repertoire of local tunes as well as many he wrote. At fiddler's contests Albert and Thornton would often take first and second, with Thornton winning first place almost as often as Albert. After years of playing together, the student was as proficient as the master.

On the second side of the *Whitetop* album, Thornton played melody to Emily's singing on three Carter Family standards: "The Storms Are on the Ocean"; "Single Girl"; and "I Never Will Marry." Thornton is featured on "Green Valley Waltz," and two fiddle tunes, "Dugannon" and "My Child Is Gonna Be a Miner," both of which he wrote. He sang lyrics to the second tune that went: "My Child's gonna be a miner / Don't care what they say / My Child is gonna be a miner / and Walk in my footsteps someday." With Flurry Dowe on both sides, all of the musicians were prominently featured.

Even after the recording, the band was not really a performance band. In the same year the album was recorded Albert appeared at the New River Festival with a group he introduced as the Poverty Gulch Band. It featured Flurry on banjo, Paul Spencer on guitar, and Johnny Sturgill on bass. There was also unidentified mandolin player on stage with them. The crowd loved Albert's portrayal of the band as a bunch of poor stragglers from "Poverty Gulch" who were trying to earn money to get home.

Shortly after the first record began to be distributed, Albert and the Spencers were inundated with requests to play festivals and make appearances at concert halls, fairs, and schools throughout the region. Almost haphazardly they solidified into a core Whitetop Mountain Band. The line-up featured Albert and Thornton on twin fiddles, Flurry on banjo, Emily on guitar and a friend from Galax, Tom Barr, often on bass. This band had the sound Albert had been looking for. It had the Whitetop

Five—The Grooming of a Banjo Player

sound. His and Thornton's driving twin fiddles could rise above the solid rhythm section and soar.

When Kyle Creed heard this configuration of the band, he implored them to record a second album, this time featuring the full band. The first recording had done well for the label and he believed a full band album could do even better. So one year after their first Mountain release, Albert and the band recorded their second album, *Cacklin' Hen*. This recording featured 12 new cuts with Emily singing four of them, two on each side. Seven of the other eight cuts featured the powerful twin fiddling of Albert and Thornton. One cut, "Whisperin' Winds," was another of Thornton's own tunes that demonstrated his virtuosity and his writing ability.

The recording sessions for this venture took place once again in Albert's living room on Cabin Creek, during weekend playing sessions that included many onlookers. Kyle would nervously dart around the house, turning off various appliances, trying to create a soundproof atmosphere. He would then hide himself in a darkened hall off the living room with his two-track recorder. Just as he flipped the recorder to "ON," he would

The Whitetop Mountain Band, 1976. Back row, from left, Flurry Dowe, Albert Hash, Thornton Spencer, Tom Barr. Front, from left, Becky Haga and Emily Spencer (photograph by Martin Fox).

grab a large utility flashlight and shine it in the eyes of the musicians as his "RECORDING" light. The small audience, and Albert, couldn't help but giggle and that led a frustrated Kyle to request several takes of each tune.[18]

With two recordings being distributed and a number of appearances at the large local festivals, Albert Hash and the Whitetop Mountain Band were gathering national attention. Flurry Dowe, who had quite literally stumbled upon the Whitetop Mountain sound in his search for "real" old-time music, could hardly believe his fortune. In four short years he had gone from being an Alabama teenager who longed to play the banjo to becoming the lead banjoist for one of the most prominent old-time bands in the nation. As Albert told one interviewer, "He [Flurry] has got the truest clawhammer lick of anybody there is. He's got the mountain clawhammer banjo." To Flurry Dowe, who would stay and play with Albert and Thornton for another four years, it all must have seemed like a Whitetop Mountain dream.

Six

Bringing Whitetop to the World

Audrey Joins the Shop

One of the great joys of Albert's life was the fact that his daughter, Audrey, had decided to join him in building instruments and work in the shop with him. Although she had been interested in her father's work since the age of three when she would sit patiently by his feet and arrange the wood scraps, she was now becoming a full-time instrument builder and began to spend most of her days and many of her evenings in her father's shop.

Fiddle building had nearly been pre-ordained in Audrey's life since her birth when Albert took the beautiful Indian-headed fiddle he had built into town and sold it to pay the doctor for her delivery. He loved to tease his daughter about that as she grew older. "I can't believe I traded such a good fiddle for a scrawny little rat like you," he would say.[1]

What goes around sometimes comes around. In 1978, after being commissioned by the Episcopal church in West Jefferson, North Carolina, to build a harp for use in its services, she was surprised. On the day the church received and blessed the harp, a member of the church walked up to Audrey and presented her with the Indian head fiddle that he had bought from Albert 29 years before, the day after Audrey was born.

As she became more interested in building instruments, Albert gently guided her work, making suggestions here and there, but always considering her a partner in his work. "Dad always told me, when we ran the shop, 'Let's give a discount to all preachers and bootleggers. 'Cause you're never gonna know which one we'll need first,'" she recalled. After Albert had given Audrey plans and wood for a mountain dulcimer when she was a teen, she had surprised him by building and selling well over a hundred of them by the time she reached her late 20s.

When she was 21, in 1970, she built her first fiddle, carefully watching her father's every step and learning the process. She was so nervous about the result that she couldn't get her hands to stop shaking long enough to put strings on the fiddle when it was done. After Albert helped her string it up and played a tune on it, she presented the crude but heartfelt instrument to her father for his birthday. She told her father, "I wanted to get you a Cadillac, but this is all I could afford." Her father, deeply touched, looked into her eyes and said, "I'd rather have this fiddle than all the Cadillacs in the world." Albert knew that this would not be his daughter's last fiddle.

As Albert's notoriety among old-time musicians and instrument collectors grew, the requests for his fiddles and his knowledge of fiddle making grew. Having Audrey in the shop was a true blessing to his work as she was already well versed in using a pocketknife to carve intricate designs and figures into instruments. She also learned the ins and outs of using her father's growing number of homemade machines.

"One time I built a fiddle with a woman on the headstock, true to daddy's fashion," said Audrey. "Well, he had never carved a fiddle head with a woman on it, so he said, 'I believe I'll make one, too.'"

"He made a beautiful carving on the headstock; a woman with long golden locks flowing down the peg head and sides of the fiddle neck," Audrey continued. "Then, when he was almost done, he looked at me and said, 'Audrey, can you help me with this hair? I ain't a beautician.'"

With Audrey beside him, Albert became very productive building not only fiddles, but also experimenting with banjos, mandolins, and new and innovative fiddle designs. Audrey would build and sell her own fiddles, which soon brought in as much cash as her dad's fiddles did, and she also found time to help her dad with intricate details on his own fiddles.

Albert's Influence Spreads

After Albert coaxed his own daughter into the craft, he began to actively recruit others, particularly young people, to learn the art of instrument building.

People like Randall Eller were often reluctant followers at first, but Albert's passion for the craft soon won them over.

Randall and his older brother were carpenters, and both were inter-

Six—Bringing Whitetop to the World

ested in woodworking and carving and lived near Chilhowie, Virginia. When they heard about a local woodcarving festival at Hungry Mother State Park one Saturday, they decided to go over and learn what they could. That is where they first encountered Albert.[2]

Albert and Audrey had a booth and were demonstrating instrument building at the festival. Albert was building a beautiful fiddle, while Audrey was undertaking a "courting" dulcimer. Courting or double dulcimers had been popular after the Civil War in southwest Virginia and were designed so that one instrument had two fret boards parallel to one another and could be played by two people at the same time. This allowed young lovers to play close together, seated across from one another. Watchful parents could listen, and if the music stopped, it might be time to intervene.

Randall was amazed when Albert took a fiddle he was building and took the top off to show him the intricacies involved. "He told me, 'If you can carve, you can make a fiddle,'" said Randall. Eller didn't know the first thing about fiddles and had only heard old-time music as a child. "You should come over to the house sometime and I'll show you how to get started," Albert told him. He gave him explicit directions to his house on Cabin Creek.

Albert and his youngest daughter, Audrey, twin fiddling a tune, ca. 1979 (courtesy Carla Osborne).

Several months later Randall and his brother were hunting and camping at a favorite spot not far from Whitetop, and it started to rain, hard. When the two young men realized their hunting was ruined for the day, Randall remembered Albert's kind offer. "We should go over and visit that Albert Hash fellow," Randall told his brother. His brother was reluctant to just drop in on someone they barely knew, but Randall was persuasive. "Let's go," he said. "It beats sittin' around here in the rain."

When they got to Albert's house the two wet hunters knocked on the door and Ethel answered. "Oh, come on in," she warmly greeted them. "He's downstairs in his shop." It felt to Randall like Albert and Ethel almost had been expecting the visit. As they walked in, Ethel had them stop at a pedestal in the living room and print their names in a proudly displayed visitor's book.

The young men headed down the stairs. When they got to the shop, they could barely make out Audrey and Albert in the clouds of cigarette smoke that filled the basement room. Albert started to show Randall all of his machines and lots of fiddles in various stages of development. Randall felt overwhelmed. "Well, I don't think I could ever do all this," he told Albert. Albert smiled. "Of course you can," he said. "You just build it one piece at a time."

The story from this point is familiar. Albert, just like he had done with Wayne Henderson and hundreds of people since, gave Randall a pattern of a fiddle back and a piece of wood. "Now you are a carver," said Albert. "Take this home and carve it, just like that, and then bring it on back and we'll get you another piece." Eller tried to pay for the wood, but Albert wouldn't hear of it. He went home and spent a month carving the back and brought it back. Albert told him it was perfect and sent him back home with plans for a top and beautiful piece of spruce.

Just like that, piece by piece, with careful instruction and lots of encouragement along the way from Albert, Randall began to see his first fiddle emerge. Before the end of the year came, Randall had a whole fiddle in his hands. Although it didn't look as smooth and delicate as one of Albert's masterpieces, it was a playable and good-looking fiddle. Today it hangs proudly in Eller's instrument shop behind his house in Chilhowie where he has built 70 fiddles, several mandolins and a few guitars as a tribute to his teacher, Albert Hash.

"I tried and tried to pay him for those lessons in fiddle building," said Randall. "He would never take a dime. So finally, I started bringing him homemade sausage and food, which he served to visitors." For Christmas,

Six—Bringing Whitetop to the World

Albert gave Randall some really good wood he had gotten in a trade, and Randall started right away on his second fiddle. Albert also gave Randall a very comprehensive book on the history of the fiddle that had a variety of patterns in the back. Nearly 40 years later, Randall is considered one of Virginia's finer craftsmen. He, like so many others, attributes his success to Albert and his generosity.

Joyce: Spreading Albert's Spirit

Albert's other daughter, Joyce, was deeply influenced by her father in other ways. She became known for her love of family and her selfless generosity, much like both her father and her mother. Though she is rarely mentioned in Albert's legacy, she embodied the best of Albert's loving kindness throughout her life.

"She was more of a behind-the-scenes gal," said her daughter, Carla Osborne. "She loved her daddy and took on his good qualities." Albert had helped Joyce build a dulcimer that she coveted and played some, but she never really got interested in working in her dad's shop.[3]

Instead, Joyce loved and devoted her energy to her family and to caring for others, especially her own children. She also loved her uncle Thornton, who spent so much time at the Hashes' house when he was young that Joyce thought he was her older brother, and Thornton acted as such. During his army years, she and Thornton wrote to one another often and she received gifts, letters and postcards from him even when he was stationed in Iceland.

Albert was a fun dad, whittling toys, playing games and generally doting on his daughters. Like her father, Joyce stayed with her grandparents, the Spencers, to attend a school that was close to them because the trek from Fees Ridge was just too far and returned home on weekends. When she married, she eloped to South Carolina. While Ethel didn't have much to say after learning about the elopement, Albert, always the true optimist, declared, "Well, now I have a son!"

Although Joyce was not as visible to others as Audrey in Albert's life, she and her children spent a great deal of time at Albert and Ethel's on Cabin Creek and enjoyed the constant flow of guests and musicians in and out of the house. Albert's mother was also always there, and if she heard of Albert heading to a music gathering or a festival, she would suddenly become quite ill and ask Albert to stay home to take care of her.

Appalachian Fiddler Albert Hash

Albert at a festival booth showcasing his and his daughter Audrey's fiddles and dulcimers (courtesy Carla Osborne).

"As kids, we were told not to mention fiddler's conventions or anything of the sort," remembered Carla Osborne. "We would go to visit and our mom would stay with Granny Reedy [Albert's mother; she remarried Thomas Reedy who had passed away by the time the grandchildren came to visit] while Albert and Ethel slipped off with The Whitetop Mountain Band to enjoy some good old time music. It provided a break for Ethel, who was Granny's full-time caretaker."

Joyce's son, David Osborne, became a frequent visitor to Albert's shop at age eight and through his grandfather developed interests in instrument making, machine building and gunsmithing. David recalled that Albert was "the best grandfather a kid could imagine." One of the things that stuck out most in David's mind was the whimsical sense of humor that he shared with everyone and his love of practical jokes.

"One day we were headed to the store in Albert's old Plymouth car. On the way, we hit a bump and the rusty old exhaust pipe broke almost in two, right below the front seat," David recalled. "When it bowed down, almost to the ground, it made that Plymouth sound like a big fancy hot rod. So Albert pulled over and wrapped a piece of wire around that pipe

Six—Bringing Whitetop to the World

and brought the wire up into the car through a hole in the floorboard and wrapped it around a bolt to hold it. Then Albert said, 'Watch this.'"

Albert proceeded to drive past the home of a local sheriff's deputy. When he got right in front of the deputy's house, which had a large picture window, Albert took the wire and dropped the pipe, making the Plymouth roar past the house. He went up the road a short distance, pulled over, and tightened the wire back up, bringing the exhaust pipe back together. They drove back down by the house peaceably, noting the deputy glaring out the window at the highway.

"Then we turned around again," David said, "and when we got to the window, no one was there, so Albert dropped that pipe again and floor boarded the Plymouth! We grandkids was eatin' it up, we were laughin' so hard[4]!"

"Why don't you build dulcimers?"

Albert's influence spread in unique ways not just to his family but also to many of his friends and acquaintances. His minister at the Lutheran church, Walt Messick, had come to Whitetop Mountain from a church in inner-city Philadelphia to the relative quiet of the mountains in 1978. He was given the responsibility of two churches, one in Whitetop and one in Konnarock. The very week he preached his first sermon, he met Albert and Ethel. Shortly after the service, Albert invited the minister to come by his house before he headed back to his home. When he got there, he couldn't believe the scene in Albert's front yard. The Rev. Messick had never heard mountain music before, let alone experienced it firsthand.[5]

There, in the front yard, was Albert, Thornton, Flurry, and at least seven or eight musicians playing what Walt called "the most beautiful music I'd ever heard." Right away, Albert drew him in and began to educate him on the Whitetop sound. "He started to take me to festivals, nearly every Saturday," Walt remembered. "It would be me, Ethel and Albert in the car. When we'd get to a festival, Albert would excitedly head off to play and leave Ethel and me in a booth or under a tarp, guarding the fiddles. It was quite an education!"

Walt remembered Albert and Ethel being in church almost every Sunday and they quickly became close friends. Although Walt ministered to two small country churches, he had a hard time making ends meet. One day in 1979, he complained to Albert about needing money and needing a part-time job. "Well, I guess you can come help me and Audrey make some instruments," replied Albert. "Why don't you just build dulcimers?"

Walt smiled. "Well, I told him, I don't play any instruments and I don't really know anything about it," said Walt, "but Albert just smiled that encouraging smile of his, and said, 'We'll teach you, Reverend.'" Walt was going to have to find a job somewhere, so without thinking much about it, he trusted the fiddler and just said, "Yes."

For the next year, Walt would head over to Albert's shop every day, after finishing his church duties, and assist Audrey in building dulcimers and fetch tools and wood for Albert. "It was a real education, there in Albert's basement," he recalled. "Not only did I learn so much from Audrey and Albert, but the conversations that went on in that shop fascinated me. Albert would string up a fiddle and someone like Thornton would play it and recommend changing the bridge position or something, and an argument would ensue. This was fascinating to me."

Over the course of the year, Walt not only became accomplished at building dulcimers and doing simple repairs to instruments, but he also came to admire Albert, his parishioner, even more. "He was one of the finest men I ever met," said Walt. "It was his whole lifestyle, the way he lived."

After finishing his year with Audrey and Albert, he built a shop behind his home and started building mountain dulcimers. In 1989, he left the ministry to go into dulcimer building full time. Since building his first instrument with Albert and Audrey, he has built nearly 1200 instruments and his company, Cabin Creek Instruments, is nationally known for its quality craftsmanship. "It's all, everything I have and know, and my quality of life, because of Albert Hash," Walt declared.

To Hollywood and Beyond

Albert's fiddles and his reputation began to travel far and wide. In January 1978, Albert received a brief missive on a postcard from Hollywood, California. On the back it simply said,

Dear Albert,

Tune in "The Waltons" on Thursday January 26th, and see the Albert Hash Fiddle. I'll be playing it. Let us hear from you.

Love Harold Hensley[6]

Six—Bringing Whitetop to the World

Hensley, a Hollywood actor and musician, had grown up in the Whitetop area and on a trip back home in the early '70s had purchased a fiddle from Albert. That fiddle had appeared in several movies and had been played on several of Hensley's recordings with well-known musicians and now was appearing on the hit TV show *The Waltons*. The influence of Whitetop music and Albert's fiddles seemed to be without boundaries.

Audrey and Albert were swamped with requests to demonstrate their skills in instrument building, just as the Whitetop Mountain Band was being inundated with requests to play in the late 1970s. They gave shows and workshops at the Virginia Folklife Festival at Ferrum College, provided music and a fiddle-making demonstration at the Smithsonian's National Folklife Festival on the National Mall in Washington, D.C., traveled to festivals in Virginia, North Carolina, West Virginia, Kentucky, and played to a sold-out crowd at Dartmouth College in northern New Hampshire.

Albert was asked to teach fiddle at the prestigious Augusta Heritage Center at Davis & Elkins College in West Virginia, at Berea College in Kentucky, and at the Wolf Trap National Performing Arts Center near Washington, D.C. In addition, Albert and the band continued to participate in the many local festivals, from the local firefighters' Ramp Festival to the fiddler's conventions in Galax, Independence, Marion and Hillsville. Albert's life had become focused on what he had hoped for, preserving the music he loved and teaching fiddle making.

The first two Whitetop Mountain recordings had also traveled far and wide. Young people from New York City like Andy Cahan who had gotten hold of the records while still in high school made an effort to travel to Grayson County in search of the Whitetop sound. Often accompanied by music enthusiast and player Paul Brown, Alice Gerrard, who was part of the duo Hazel and Alice (with Hazel Dickens), and self-declared folklorist and history teacher Ray Alden, Andy would lead the trek up the winding road to Albert's house on Cabin Creek.

"They made us feel right away like part of the family," Paul Brown recalled.[7] "Albert and Ethel were always welcoming." Paul had come to learn as much as he could about fiddle construction while the others wanted Albert to play tunes that they could record. Albert patiently obliged each of them and they always left feeling like they had not only learned something about Albert's craft, but they had also learned something about themselves. "He always had a way of making you feel good about yourself," said Cahan.[8]

Andy had come to visit the area during college, infatuated with all of its music, especially the fiddling of Earnest East. Due to an amazing series of events at the age of 21, Andy found himself moving to the area and playing banjo in Earnest's band, the Pine Ridge Boys, with Earnest's son and daughter-in-law.

At one of the first festivals he played, Andy met Albert and the rest of the Whitetop Mountain Band which had recently added another guitar player and singer, Becky Haga, who would later marry bass player Tom Barr. Andy was already familiar with the band from the first two albums he had bought in New York. "I was just blown away," recalled Andy. "They were just the tightest, smoothest old-time band I had ever seen live."

Andy met Albert that day, and like so many others, promptly received an invitation to visit at his home. Andy made many trips up the winding road to Cabin Creek. He remembered, "As you headed up that road, it became more and more beautiful and more remote. I thought that Albert's house was one of the prettiest places I had been. And then, they were so kind to me, so welcoming."

Paul Brown, a long-time player, collector and disseminator of old-time music, was living in Galax and working for WPAQ Radio in Mt. Airy, North Carolina, a unique station that was founded by old-time enthusiast Ralph Epperson. Epperson had started the station in his parents' bedroom,

Joyce Hash Osborne with her granddaughter, Emily Clark, 1998. Joyce embodied Albert's kindness, compassion and caring (courtesy Carla Osborne).

Six—Bringing Whitetop to the World

and from its inception he used the airwaves to celebrate the music of the Blue Ridge Mountains. Paul, who had migrated to the area after college in Ohio, was known for his association studying the music of North Carolina fiddler Tommy Jarrell. After hearing often about Albert from Tommy, who admired Albert's fiddling in contests and performances, Paul had decided to visit Albert himself.

"Albert had a clear, 'notey,' distinctive style of fiddling," recalled Paul. "He followed melody very carefully, in ways other fiddlers did not. He was somewhere in between the old Galax fiddling of Emmet Lundy and Luther Davis and people like Tommy Jarrell and Norman Edmonds. You could hear the influence of Arthur Smith and Grayson, but it was really just Albert. He had his own way of playing that told you where he was from," Paul said.

Picking a Fiddle

One visitor to Albert's basement shop, record producer and musician Bobby Patterson, described his visit as if "we'd walked down into that basement and it was just like a termite workin' in sawdust heaven."[9] Other visitors, who were all asked to sign the guest book, were overcome by the

From left, Albert, Thornton, and the banjo player they carefully groomed, Flurry Dowe, ca. 1975 (photograph by Mark Sanderford).

grandfather clock that filled the living room. One bedroom in the house was often full of fiddles of every kind, some Albert had built and some he'd bartered for.

One young fiddler, Sam Gobble, who came to Albert's shop looking for a new fiddle, was given the grand tour. "After showing me all around the shop," Sam said, "then he took me up to a spare bedroom where there were 30 or 40 fiddles laid out on the bed. He had either built or repaired all of them." Sam didn't have a lot of money at the time, so he told Albert his price range. "Well," Albert told him, "you can take about most any fiddle here, but I recommend this one." Albert grabbed a fiddle from the middle of the bed. Sam could tell Albert was trying hard to match him up with a fiddle.

After trying several fiddles and spending an hour or so looking, Sam decided on another fiddle. Albert was a bit taken aback that he didn't select the one he had picked for Sam but made sure the fiddle he'd picked was set up to his liking and sent him on his way. After a several weeks, the fiddle Sam had bought developed some problems, so he took it back to Albert for repair. Albert felt bad and told him he could have his pick of the fiddles still on display in the bedroom or he could just leave the fiddle he had bought and Albert would fix it. Once again, Albert picked the exact same fiddle he had recommended for Sam earlier from the bed and put it in his hands. This time, Sam decided to take the fiddle home, since Albert seemed to be convinced it was the right fiddle for him. Today, more than 40 years later, Sam still owns and plays that fiddle.

The Band Records

By 1979, the Whitetop Mountain Band, featuring Albert and Thornton and his wife Emily as well as Tom Barr and Becky Haga (who would later become Tom's wife), was ready to record the band's third record album. Kyle Creed, whose health was beginning to fail with cancer, had sold his Mountain Records label to his business partner, Bobby Patterson. Bobby, who knew Albert and Thornton well, encouraged the group to head into Galax and record this record in the studio where Bobby would have more control.

"When Albert and Thornton came into the studio, they were all business," Bobby recalled. "Thornton, especially, wanted to make sure everything was right. Albert was just as he always was, just the most hum-

Six—Bringing Whitetop to the World

ble man you've ever met. The band played just perfect. They pretty much nailed every track the first time through." The new album featured 14 tracks, seven of which featured the twin fiddling of Albert and Thornton, and seven others that featured Emily and Becky's singing. By now, Bobby's label, Heritage Records, was well known and widely distributed by Dave Freeman who had created County Sales in Floyd, Virginia, a unique record distribution service for old-time and bluegrass music. Freeman's presence at all of the major and minor old-time festivals ensured wide distribution of the record among old-time fans.

Thumpin' the Wood

The band's notoriety also attracted the notice of the National Forest Service. It was producing a documentary film on Virginia forests and recruited Albert and the band to provide a soundtrack. Albert, a shrewd barterer, requested that in exchange for the services, he and the band be given access to some Appalachian spruce trees that needed to be thinned on Whitetop Mountain. This was one of the few remaining red spruce forests in the state, and ultimately the deal insured that Albert, Tom Barr (who was also building fiddles) and their good friend Wayne Henderson would have a local supply of the coveted instrument building wood for years to come.

In 1982, popular musician and PBS host David Holt brought his nationally broadcast show *Folkways* to Whitetop Mountain for an installment of the show that featured mountain instrument makers. Following a talk with banjo and mountain dulcimer maker Stanley Hicks, David brought his crew to Albert's shop to feature Albert's playing and fiddle making.

Albert told David the story of his first fiddle and played a few tunes for the camera. David then asked Albert about the spruce he used for the top. With a straight face and a wry smile, Albert told David and his national PBS audience, "You will examine maybe a dozen trees before you find the right one." Then, sitting on his front porch steps, Albert told David and his camera crew what he did when he went up to the top of Whitetop Mountain hunting fiddle tops.

"You have to take a large rock and walk up and down the spruce banging on them." The camera caught Albert mimicking whacking a large spruce with a rock, the sound of the hit echoing off the mountain. "When you hear the right one it will have a hollow sound and that thud will echo up and down the mountains." Holt, who totally bought Albert's story, asked him, "You can hear it even with the bark on it?" Albert, without missing a beat, replied, "Yes," and continued to embellish the story. One only wonders how many budding fiddle builders have been seen since beating spruce trees with rocks in the Appalachian woodlands.[10]

The Carter Fold

One venue that Albert and the Whitetop Mountain Band played often was about an hour and a half from Whitetop in the small town of Hiltons, Virginia. The Carter Family Fold, in Poor Valley, was home to Sara and A.P. Carter and the home base of the original Carter Family, pioneers of modern country music. On the grounds are the tiny cabin in which the Carters lived and A.P.'s store. In 1977, Janette Carter, one of A.P. and Sara's three daughters, established it as one of the most popular venues in the South to hear original old-time and bluegrass music. One of their favorite bands was the Whitetop Mountain Band as attested to in a letter Janette wrote to Albert in 1978:

> *Dear Albert,*
>
> *How are you? I can give you March 24th—your band and Wayne Henderson—I feel you all work well together and break all the hoe down music down the same.*
>
> *You are one of the most requested bands we have in the old time category. Write me a yes or no to this date.*
>
> *Janette Carter*[11]

Albert loved to play at the Carter Fold. Janette was always a gracious hostess, paying the band well and encouraging Albert to tantalize the crowd with his trick fiddling and the band's great driving rhythm always attracted the local flatfooting crowd.

Grandpa Albert

Ethel, Albert's wife, was still caring for Albert's mother and had increasing responsibilities for her own parents, both of whom were suffering with ailments related to aging. In addition, Ethel would good naturedly welcome her daughters, her grandchildren, and visitors from every corner of the earth into her living room, cooking for, cleaning up after and helping to entertain them all. By this time, Albert's mother rarely left her bedroom, but visitors recall her often contributing to conversations in the living room, listening from her adjacent bedroom to every word and chiming in when she saw fit.

All three of Albert's brothers continued to visit, as did his daughters and the grandchildren, who were constantly underfoot. Albert and Ethel enjoyed showing their relatives a good time, hosting music parties in their honor and hiking with them on Whitetop Mountain and the surrounding hills. Carla Osborne remembered one of the roads he liked to take them on, "Straight Branch," one of the most twisted, crooked and wash-boarded roads in the area.

One day when Albert had Carla and the grandkids out for a walk, a frustrated tourist stopped Albert on the main road and asked angrily, "Do you know the fastest way out of these @#%$* mountains?" The grandchildren gasped, wondering what their grandpa was going to do. Albert didn't miss a beat. He gave a wry smile to the children and said, "Sure," then

Albert in his basement shop on Cabin Creek, ca. 1981 (photograph by Mark Sanderford).

proceeded to instruct the driver directly down Straight Branch road. The grandchildren tried to harness their giggles.

The grandchildren always enjoyed the many visitors to Albert and Ethel's house and enjoyed the British, Irish and German accents of the visitors who had traveled from across the world to meet the Fees Branch fiddler. Albert was careful to include them in the conversations and would often have the visitors show the children where they were from on a map. "We always got an education of some sort when we visited our grandpa and granny," recalled Carla.

The Music Program

Albert continued to enter fiddle contests and to be featured at festivals and music schools across the Blue Ridge region. Increasingly, he began to worry that there weren't enough youngsters wanting to learn the music. The "folkies" that had started visiting him in the late '60s and early '70s were getting older, and fewer caravans of young people, eager to learn, traveled to Albert's door. Albert worried that the Whitetop sound wasn't going to be passed down because not many local young people seemed to be interested in playing the local music.

He talked with Thornton and Emily and his daughter Audrey about his concern and Emily pointed out that there wasn't even a music program at the school that Albert had attended, Mt. Rogers High School. In fact, it turned out that when Albert and Audrey went to talk to the principal, Mrs. Wilma Testerman, about starting a school music program, the only instrument the school owned was an old, out-of-tune piano that a few of the teachers could play.

Mrs. Testerman, who had been at the school as a teacher for more than 20 years, had recently become principal when the local mail carrier had knocked on her classroom door and handed her the keys to the school, saying, "Here, Wilma, you're the principal." She hadn't even been informed that her predecessor had retired.

Wanting to make some positive changes to help her students, Mrs. Testerman had desperately wanted the children at Mt. Rogers to have a more well-rounded education and music was a big part of what she saw in her students' futures.

When Albert and Audrey met with the school staff, they brainstormed some ways to get a program started and how to deal with the issue of cre-

Six—Bringing Whitetop to the World

Albert and his granddaughters wearing hats and trying to frown for an "old timey" photograph, ca. 1981–82. Back row, from left, Carla Osborne and Beth Miller. Front row, from left, Amanda Miller Coldiron, Albert, and Rachel Osborne. Amanda and Beth were Audrey's daughters. This was the bowler hat that Albert later gave to Thornton Spencer who wore it nearly every time he performed (courtesy Carla Osborne).

dentialing the program. Together, Albert and his family decided to start their own music program for the young people in the Whitetop area. They would hold lessons after school, at the Mt. Rogers fire station, for free, open to any of the young people who wanted to attend.

To make sure it would be accepted, they carefully planned to introduce the idea to a council meeting in Konnarock to receive the proper permissions to use the firehouse and to sanction the program. Mrs. Testerman had organized the ad hoc music committee's attendance at the big meeting. On that night, Albert in his church-going sport coat, Audrey in a dress, Mrs. Testerman in her school dress, a local council member, Hazel Price, in a business suit, and a very refined, well-dressed and distinguished but aged member of the council that none of them knew loaded into Mrs. Testerman's car to go to the meeting.

About five minutes into the trip up and down the winding road to Konnarock, something in Hazel Price's handbag began to rattle loudly. To

The original Mt. Rogers School that Albert attended for high school. Later a larger wing was added when it became the Mt. Rogers Combined School incorporating lower grades. It now stands empty on Hwy 58 (photograph by Jim Kacsmarik).

this day no one knows what she had in there, but Albert and Mrs. Testerman exchanged a quick smile at the rattle. Suddenly, the distinguished older gentleman blurted out, "Mrs. Testerman, are you sure there isn't a rattlesnake in this car?"

Albert, Audrey and Wilma Testerman began to giggle, each of them covering their mouths to not embarrass the gentleman. When they finally reached the meeting house and piled out of the car, Albert and Wilma let loose with uncontrollable laughter at the idea of the rattlesnake. As Wilma tried to compose herself and head into the meeting, Albert grabbed her arm, looked at her quite seriously and burst forth with "Don't you start in there 'til I get over this!" The two clutched each other, laughing hysterically, before finally heading in and successfully presenting the music program to the council.

The music committee put the word out in the community that they needed instruments—guitars, fiddles and banjos—and got a quick response. Thornton, Emily, and Audrey all volunteered to teach groups and individual lessons and Albert recruited an extra guitar teacher from nearby Konnarock, Lorene Grim, to accommodate the number of guitar students that enrolled. Lorene's help came with a catch, though: If Albert wanted her to teach in the program, her two children, Brian and Debbie, who were both seven, would have to be enrolled in classes. Of course, Albert agreed.

The Konnarock Kritters

"Albert just kind of took me under his wing," recalled Brian Grim. "Albert showed me how to hold my fiddle. Then he would play a tune real slow. I would stare at his fingers until I felt like I could play with him. Some days, Thornton would teach fiddle and he broke it down more. I would hear the two of them talkin' about me, sayin', 'I don't know whether that boy is gonna get it or not.' One day, it just hit me," said Brian, "and Albert's style of bowing just all of a sudden felt natural."[12]

The Mt. Rogers Volunteer Fire Department where music lessons for local students began (photograph by Jim Kacsmarik).

When Albert and Thornton saw that Brian was going to become a fiddler, that he was getting it, they celebrated. "Neither one of them ever said a discouraging word or put us down in any way. It was just pure encouragement, and I desperately wanted to please them, but most of all, I wanted it for myself," said Brian.

Emily was teaching banjo at the firehouse lessons because Flurry Dowe had realized that being a renowned old-time banjo player in rural Grayson County was never going to afford him the finer things in life. "I was tired of living in abject poverty," recalled Flurry, and after a legacy of recordings and performances with the Whitetop Mountain Band, moved on, rarely playing the banjo again. In 1979 he moved to Blacksburg and enrolled in Virginia Tech. After college, he left Virginia for the West Coast where today he raises money for the Democratic Party in California and experiences a totally different lifestyle than he did in Grayson County.

Emily had taken a keen interest in banjo and, like Flurry, had studied the playing of Jont Blevins. She had often accompanied Flurry to visit Jont or participated in jams with him at the Spencers' store and soaked up all she could from the last remaining curator of the Whitetop Mountain clawhammer style. She soon took over Flurry's role as the banjo player for the Whitetop Mountain Band, and she continues that role to this day. She also taught both banjo and guitar at the fire station. One of her first students was Brian's sister, Debbie.

"It was a great class. We had lots of guest teachers in our classes," remembered Debbie. "People like Enoch Rutherford would come up to the firehouse and show us licks, Dee Dee Price taught us some advanced classes. It was a great experience." The firehouse became a "nest" for the students who would jam after class with their teachers, learning mountain music firsthand. The firehouse was also the scene of three or four local festivals each year and all of the students would perform onstage with Albert, Thornton, Emily and others. The students were very popular with the crowds.

When Brian and Debbie Grim were about 13, their mother organized them into a band, the Konnarock Country Critters. The band featured Debbie on banjo and guitar, Brian on fiddle, their mother Lorene on guitar and Bob Reedy on bass. The group became very popular not just at the fire station but also at all the local festivals. By the time they were 17, the Grims recorded their first cassette, *Albert Taught Us to Love Old Time Music*. Suddenly, these young people were becoming very popular at festivals, dances and performances across the region.

Six—Bringing Whitetop to the World

Undated photograph of Albert giving a music lesson to Brian Grim, who would go on to lead the Konnarock Critters, one of the nation's most popular old-time bands (courtesy Debbie Grim Yates).

As Brian aged, he fully developed his ability to emulate Albert's bowing style. "It was circular bowing," said Brian. "Somehow it just felt natural to me. I have tried to teach it to others and a few have gotten on to it. It is a unique and very powerful style. You can drive that fiddle with that Albert Hash down bow, you can get the power out of it." Brian's bowing and Debbie's banjo playing, rooted in the Grayson County sound of elders like Albert, Thornton, Jont Blevins, Enoch Rutherford, and Emily Spencer, soon took off so well that the twin Grims became the talk of old-time music across the nation.

They slowly evolved out of the "Country" and into just the "Konnarock Critters," and Jim Lloyd took over for their mother on guitar. They developed a powerful, fast, and recognizable sound, driven by Brian's Albert-like fiddling and Debbie's dynamic banjo attack. The Critters became a favorite at both old-time and bluegrass festivals nationwide. Before they stopped to raise their own families, they would go on to make more than five studio recordings and CDs, play across the United States, make two tours of Europe and carry Albert's tradition of Whitetop fiddling to a whole new generation of young musicians.

Albert performing with the Konnarock Country Critters, Debbie and Brian Grim, 1980 (courtesy Debbie Grim Yates).

A Model Program

The style and structure of the firehouse lessons seemed to work well. Many of those first students, like the Grims, became well versed in old-time music and many went on to perform professionally or to teach traditional music themselves. The method—formal individual or small group lessons followed by informal jams in which the students could demonstrate their new tunes and skills in a group setting, followed by community performances—really has become the most widely used methodology in folk music teaching.

Six—Bringing Whitetop to the World

The Konnarock Critters at Dollywood, 1990. Back row, from left, Terry Semones, Sam Paine, and Jim Lloyd. Front row, Brian and Debbie Grim (courtesy Debbie Grim Yates).

After Albert's death, the firehouse lessons became so widely admired that they were adopted as part of the school curriculum at Mt. Rogers School. Emily Spencer was hired as a full-time music teacher to teach traditional instruments and traditional music to the area's students. Under her supervision, the students formed the Albert Hash Memorial Band, a traveling ensemble that has been featured at concerts and events across Virginia.

The model that Albert started to teach the mountain children about their musical heritage was adopted and slightly modified by a friend of Wayne Henderson's, Helen White, who would found the nonprofit JAM (Juniors Appalachian Musicians) program with some counsel from Emily and others. Sprouting from the seed Albert planted at the firehouse, JAMs now provides after-school lessons to thousands of kids in the fourth through the eighth grades in Virginia, Kentucky, North Carolina, South Carolina and Tennessee.

The programs offer lessons in fiddle, guitar, mandolin, banjo and other mountain instruments as well as traditional dance classes. JAM students and JAM bands are regularly featured at festivals across the region. The JAM program incorporates the spirit and structure of the firehouse lessons pioneered by Albert at Whitetop.[13]

Whitetop at the World's Fair

In 1981, Albert received an invitation to play at the 1982 World's Fair in Knoxville, Tennessee. At first, he saw this as a real opportunity to share the Whitetop sound with people from all over and was excited for the opportunity. He was a bit disappointed, however, when the exhibition hall where they played featured cut-outs of hillbillies and drawings that looked like they had come from a Mountain Dew advertisement. He felt that his beloved mountain music was being depicted as a novelty played by ignorant hill folk, rather than the intricate, proud, historical tradition that was played by those with the self-reliant pioneer spirit of the mountains that he embodied.

Albert had been asked to play on several stages and he and Audrey had also been asked to demonstrate instrument building. The fair's organizers wanted him to sell his fiddles and they wanted to set the price for any instrument that Albert sold. When he heard the price the fair wanted to charge for his instruments, he refused. "Musicians can't afford that," Albert told them.[14]

Albert did perform at the fair, on several stages during the week, with his own band and with many regional musicians including Kentucky fiddler J.P. Fraley. During his main performance Thornton, Emily, and some Whitetop Mountain Band regulars backed him up. He amazed the thou-

Six—Bringing Whitetop to the World

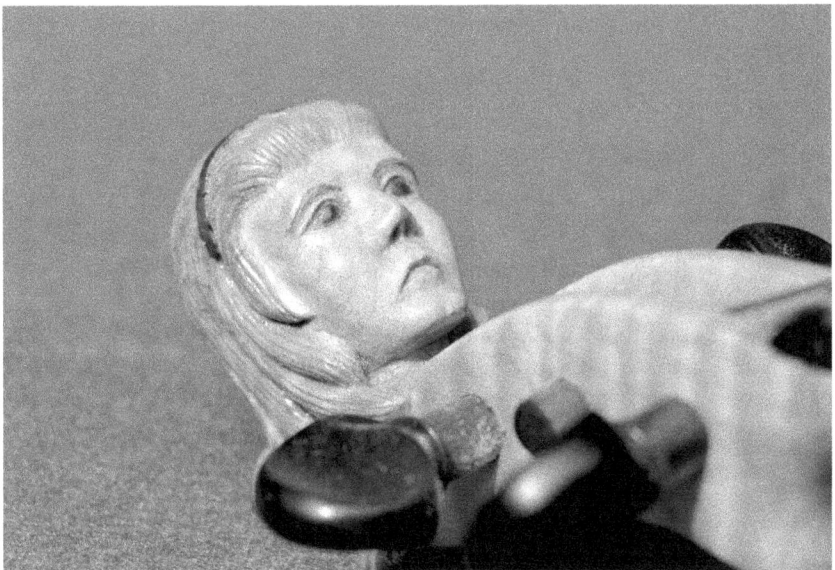

The hand carved headstock on one of the fiddles Albert built to display at the Knoxville World's Fair in 1982. This would be one of his last fiddles.

sands of fair goers who heard his main performance, playing "Turkey in the Straw" with the fiddle behind his back, an old trick he often did on stage.

In spite of the World's Fair's shortcomings, Albert was proud to represent the musical traditions of his beloved Whitetop Mountain before an international audience. The fans at the rural music stage adored him and his fiddles.

The Leaf Begins Its Fall

Albert's health was never what one would consider "strong." Throughout his life he had remained frail and was plagued by bouts of heart weakness and lung trouble. Albert had started smoking as a teenager and continued to smoke all of his life. As he reached his 60s his lungs and heart began to be seriously compromised. Although his health problems rarely slowed him down, Ethel and his family were often worried about him.

Shortly before the World's Fair, Albert had been driving a car loaded with band members, heading to a gig in the mountains. Suddenly, a small boy who had been playing in his driveway accidently sent his ball sailing into the road. Albert slammed on the brakes, and the boy hit the side of the car and fell down, escaping serious injury. The boy's parents came running down the hill, livid at Albert and those in the car and frantic about their son. The boy got up and, except for a few tears, was fine, but Albert was badly shaken.

He worried and fretted over the incidents for weeks. He could not help but imagine the fate that almost befell the young ball chaser. Mark Sanderford, a photographer, schoolteacher, and close friend of Albert's, remembered seeing Albert shortly after the incident.[15] "His eyes were bloodshot like he hadn't been sleeping, his blood pressure was sky high, and as he told me about the incident, he was visibly shaken." Though we will never know for sure, Sanderford wonders if this incident may have been the beginning of the end of Albert's life. In his frail state, the near-accident and the scolding by the child's parents weighed heavily upon him.

"The Gentle Genius." A pencil drawing of Albert by Willard Gayheart, a famous Galax artist and musician (used by permission of artist).

Shortly after the beginning of 1983, Albert Hash was taken out of his home shop and driven down the mountain to the hospital in Jefferson, North Carolina. His heart was in serious trouble, and he had suffered a heart attack. Walt Messick, who had been Albert's minister and had apprenticed in his shop, heard right away that Albert had been hospitalized. He visited Albert at the hospital the next day.

"There were people lined up to visit him. The crowd was exhausting, but

Six—Bringing Whitetop to the World

Albert welcomed everyone," said Walt. Musicians serenaded him, people came and just sat in silence, others just wanted to hold his hands.[16]

The folks who came to the hospital represented the many branches on which Albert's life in the mountains had hung. They were, of course, friends and family; neighbors who had often been touched by Albert's kindness; musicians who had learned the unique Whitetop sound from Albert; instrument builders who owed their craft to Albert's instruction and guidance; young people like Debbie and Brian Grim who had been touched by Albert's teaching; folklorists; former coworkers and a variety of mountain folk whose lives had somehow or another been affected by the breadth and depth of Albert's short life. And then there were his fans, people who had never met Albert but who had faithfully followed him and the Whitetop Mountain band to flatfoot and listen to this amazing fiddler.

Albert Hash was just 64 years old. Through his music, his skills as a luthier and machinist, his kindness and his simple way of living on the planet, he had touched thousands of others' lives.

Seven

The Last Leaf on the Tree

COMMONWEALTH OF VIRGINIA
GENERAL ASSEMBLY
HOUSE RESOLUTION NO. 18
Mourning the death of Albert L. Hash

WHEREAS, Albert L. Hash, a gifted member of the Whitetop community, died on January 28, 1983; and

WHEREAS, Albert L. Hash learned to play the fiddle when he was ten years old and became good enough to form his own band and play competitively; and

WHEREAS, Mr. Hash, a retired machinist, began building his own musical instruments and designed and constructed machines for building fiddles; and

WHEREAS, Albert Hash took great interest in the children of his community, teaching those who wanted to play the fiddle and lending a fiddle of his own to those who could not afford one; and

WHEREAS, Albert Hash helped to organize a string band at Mount Rogers schools and taught fiddle playing at Wilkes Community College in West Jefferson, N.C. as well as at the Mount Rogers Fire Department and Rescue Squad in Whitetop; and

WHEREAS, Mr. Hash gained national recognition when he performed and displayed his work at the 1982 World's Fair in Knoxville, Tennessee, and when his work was displayed at the Smithsonian Institute; now, therefore, be it

RESOLVED, by the House of Delegates, That it is fitting that the General Assembly should express its regret and sorrow upon the loss of such a talented and valuable Virginian, and be it

RESOLVED FURTHER, That Albert L. Hash's contributions to country music and to the young people of his community be duly recognized and commended; and, be it

RESOLVED FINALLY, That the Clerk of the House of Delegates prepare a copy of this resolution for presentation to Mrs. Ethel Spencer Hash as a tribute to the memory of her husband.

Agreed to by the House of Delegates
February 26, 1983

Seven—The Last Leaf on the Tree

Albert Lillard Hash passed away on January 28, 1983, at the hospital in Jefferson, North Carolina, surrounded by family and friends. The news spread quickly through the mountains, down the ridge to Galax and even to the state capital in Richmond, where the House of Delegates honored him. Following the reading of the resolution, reprinted above, the entire membership of the Virginia House of Delegates took a moment of silence in Albert Hash's honor.

Wisps of snow blew across the crest of Haw Orchard Mountain and sung through the red spruce, wrapping around Faith Lutheran Church where Albert lay at rest in a simple wooden casket. Despite the cold of that late January afternoon in Whitetop, Virginia, the crowd that had gathered to pay their final respects was spilling out into the churchyard. After solemn greetings and settling into the old wooden pews, the congregation bowed their heads as the Reverend Walter Messick began the service with a prayer[1]:

> God our Father, you are a refuge and a strength for us, a helper close at hand in times of distress. We ask you to help us now so to hear the words of our faith that our fears are dispelled, our grief is consoled, our loneliness is eased and our

Faith Lutheran Church near Whitetop where Walt Messick delivered Albert's memorial service (photograph by Jim Kacsmarik).

hope is reawakened. May the Hoy Spirit somehow lift us from the very depths of the horrible feelings we now have at Albert's death. Please lift us to the peace and calm of your enfolding love that we might continue our pilgrimage on earth in confidence until by your call, we are reunited with those who have gone on before us, through your son, Jesus Christ our Lord. Amen.

As everyone opened their eyes, Walt turned their attention to a congregant, Smith Greer, and recalled a past Sunday morning. "At one of our worship services some time ago, Smith Greer dedicated the hymn 'Just as I Am' to Albert. It brought joyful tears to his eyes and he said it was one of his favorite hymns."

Walt invited Smith to play the old hymn once more as the congregation listened in reverent silence. The hymn ended in fitting tribute to the Last Leaf on the Tree:

> Just as I am—of that free love
> The breadth, length, depth, and height to prove,
> Here for a season, then above,
> O Lamb of God, I come!

After the music, Walt led the congregation in a reading of the 23rd Psalm, scripture that Albert knew by heart. And then the funeral sermon began.

> We are here today to say goodbye to a good and dear friend. Albert Hash is one of those exceptional and rare individuals who make tracks on this earth once in a great while. Most communities have a few individuals who stand out for any number of reasons—whether it be as a leader, outspoken critic, outlaw, hard worker or whatever. There are a *few* people who stand out above all others for some reason. Albert Hash is one of those individuals. In fact, Albert is the most exceptional person to walk these mountains since the legendary Wilburn Waters of the 1800s. I believe that is why so many of us are here today.
>
> Every person is a living story. Our lives tell a story—who we are, what we stand for, our values, what we do and don't do, our standing in the community and the like. Albert's life is a best seller. It has all the ingredients for good reading—adventure, love, a man for all seasons and all people, insight into the meaning of life, self-respect, success, happiness, and contentment. Albert's book of life is captivating because as we come in contact with it, it has a way of bringing the best out of us. It is a book that teaches and encourages us to find and make our own what that banner hanging on the wall proclaims—love, joy and peace.

There was hardly a dry eye to be found in upper Grayson County the morning of Albert's funeral. While the Rev. Messick proceeded to tell the story of Albert's life, a life filled with music, machines, family, friends and fun, many in attendance looked at their own lives and realized that without this wry, slender, simple yet brilliant mountain man their own existence would be much less rich and robust. Albert's legacy would be felt in their music, the instruments they built, their kind treatment of one another, and in their respect for the traditions of the Blue Ridge Mountains.

Walt went on to identify what, to him, were the seven key themes in the life of the real self-made and self-reliant "hillbilly" who was Albert Hash.

Humility

Humility was the first theme he identified. "Albert had no problem with an inflated ego," remembered Walt. "He didn't need fame, power or material wealth. He never asked for credit. This past summer Albert was invited to the World's Fair twice: Once to display his instruments and once to perform with his band. On his trip to display his fiddles he was outraged that the Fair wanted to mark the price of his instruments up way beyond what he thought they were worth. So he refused to sell them even though he would have made a good profit. He never once advertised his talents and skills, but people like you and I flooded to his house almost daily in search of this humble man's extraordinary talents." Most of those in attendance nodded, remembering their own personal pilgrimages to Cabin Creek, Fees Branch, or Albert's school bus shop in Lansing, North Carolina.

In the 1970s a group of students from Appalachian State University interviewed Albert, and after about an hour, one young woman said to him, "Now I want you to tell us how you became famous."

Albert's reply was honest: "WHAT? I didn't know I was."

"Oh," said the student, "I read about you all the time, we all read about you."

Albert thought for a minute and said, in typical humble fashion, "Oh, I guess I'm just different from other people, that's all. I'm not famous, no." When the student interviewers insisted, Albert went on, "Oh, I've lived up here a long time, young'uns. That's about the best explanation I can have. Maybe a lot of people know me."

The students weren't satisfied. "Well, how did they find you?" one young woman asked.

Albert paused and replied, "I just happened to be at the wrong place at the right time or something. Oh, I used to go out and play at the fiddler's conventions. That's one good way they learn you. I played I wouldn't have any idea how many fiddler's conventions, you know." He also mentioned the hundreds of fairs and festivals where he and his fiddles had been featured. When asked about an upcoming invitation to show his clock and fiddle work at the Smithsonian Institution in Washington, Albert told the students that "they [the Smithsonian staff] kinda have to start a day ahead of time to find me up here." He was always humble, and his humility delighted his interviewers.[2]

Generosity

Generosity was the second chapter that Walt identified in Albert's book of life.

"He gave of himself in so many ways. He played music throughout the region to help many needs and causes, mostly at his own expense. He

A true mountain gentleman, Albert Hash, ca. 1981 (photograph by Mark Sanderford).

Seven—The Last Leaf on the Tree

taught so many people how to play old-time fiddle free of charge. And one of the things that made him such a good teacher was that he was generous with his praise of his fledgling students. They might make the most horrible noise you ever heard, but he would encourage them, have a good word to say and pat them on the back. His generous praise brought out the best in his students," Walt said.

"He shared his shop with many, giving his time, supplies and anything he had to help the person. For the last year or so of his life he personally gave me everything he had to give almost every day of the week as I worked with him and Audrey in his shop. I can't begin to tell you how generous and self-giving this man was. I couldn't begin to count the number of instruments he gave and loaned to students, and even more the number of instruments he repaired and re-repaired for students and anyone for that matter. He gave and gave until his own life gave out," Walt continued, as he fought back tears.

Pastor Messick meditated on his own year learning how to make dulcimers in Albert and Audrey's shop. He remembered how he had observed Albert being repeatedly interrupted, nearly every day, by people who wanted Albert to teach them, help them, or to build something for them. And he remembered how selflessly he gave to them of his knowledge, his gentle spirit, his tools, or his magnificent skill. He remembered how Albert had given away fiddles to those who could not afford to buy them, after the hundreds of hours Walt had watched him labor over his work bench to build each one; how he and Ethel always offered food to those who had traveled far, even as they lived on a fixed income and cared for family members; and how he always had time to play a few tunes for a tune seeker, folklorist, or curious tourist who happened by, even though he had work in his shop waiting.

Archie Powers, who had met Albert when he was a boy and had been friends with him since, once recalled how the strength of Albert's generosity drew him to hike up the mountain. "Lord, I walked from here in Lansing up Fees Ridge in the snow to see Albert. He was the most honest person I ever met," he remembered. "You could make a mistake doing something, and he could even make you feel good about it. That's the truth. He had a knack for that; make you feel good about everything. And he never seen a stranger. He helped everybody that needed help, he helped them."[3]

In the funeral crowd, Wayne Henderson smiled to himself at the notion of Albert's generosity. It was a lesson he had learned well from the day he came to Albert for advice on his first guitar. He never forgot Albert's generosity or the time he took to guide him in his quest for the perfect guitar. In turn, Albert's generosity was a gift that Wayne had returned to many others in his life, always available for charity, always taking the time, when needed, to give of his talents to others, including even Eric Clapton.

Albert's generosity had, by the time of his death, become legendary. Many mountain musicians and luthiers had taken Albert's generous way of sharing his talents to heart. Albert's lessons were never just about learning a skill or a craft; they were lessons on how to live an artistic life. Those who knew and loved Albert live by his example, taking time to teach in the growing Junior Appalachian Musicians program or sharing their skills in instrument building, their shops and their collections of precious wood with those who crave to build their own, just as Albert did.

Talent

The third virtue identified by Walt in Albert's chapter book was talent. While most of those gathered knew of Albert's great accomplishments as a fiddler and builder of fine instruments, there was more to Albert's list of talents. "We all know about his fiddle playing and instrument making. They are indeed legendary," Walt said. "He was also a master machinist by trade, an inventor, creator, repairman of what others couldn't fix, problem solver and had the unique ability to dream an idea and then to create that idea. The tools in his shop stand as a testimony to that talent. But he was talented in other areas too. He had the ability to relate to others whoever they were. He was patient, kind and loving—truly talents to be emulated."

There was no real secret to Albert's immense talents, and yet there was a secret. He attributed what talent he would humbly admit to having to thousands of hours of hard work, to his persistence and commitment. And it was true. Albert had started whittling wood and playing fiddle from before the age of 10 and he had spent a good part of nearly every day of the following 55 years doing both. He had clearly spent the 10,000 hours that author Malcolm Gladwell purported in his famous book *Outliers* that it takes to induce "mastery" of a talent or skill.[4] He had devoted significant portions of his life to "getting it right," whether it be fiddle building, gunsmithing, building clocks or playing music. However, there seemed, to everyone who knew him, to be something else about Albert that made him great.

Seven—The Last Leaf on the Tree

"He was the only genius I've ever really known," said Dean Sturgill, Albert's cousin and admirer. "He could see a fiddle or even a clock in a plain block of wood and then carve everything away that didn't belong until it took the shape he had for it."[5]

"He could do anything, I believed," said Jerry Smith, who was an engineer at Sprague Electric and worked closely with Albert for years. "If someone needed a machine, with no formal training and with only a high

The artist at work: Albert playing fiddle at the Blue Ridge Folklife Festival at Ferrum College in Ferrum, Virginia, 1980 (courtesy Carla Osborne).

school education, Albert would design it, make a working prototype, and then build it. There just weren't too many like him."[6]

Albert's musical talent was admired far and wide. Paul Brown, a noted radio host and music historian, recounted, "You could walk into a room with 10 fiddlers and you would know when it was Albert's turn. His style was his own, distinct, powerful and beautiful." Brown recalls that another admirer of Albert's unique style of fiddling was master old-time musician Tommy Jarrell. "Tommy was well aware of Albert, having heard him at many fiddler's contests and festivals, and Tommy had great admiration for Albert's playing and for Albert as a person," said Brown.[7]

Albert's immense talents in the field of native Appalachian music had taken him from the peak of Whitetop's music festival in the '30s into homes across the region by radio in the '50s and '60s to stages at Brandywine, the National Folk Festival in Washington, D.C., Wolftrap and the Carter Family Fold in his native hill country. The fiddles he built were much sought after in his lifetime and have been displayed by museums and music centers across the nation. His talent continues to inspire young fiddlers through his recordings and his fiddles are emulated by many current-day Virginia builders like Chris Testerman, Randall Eller and many others.

Respect for Others

The fourth chapter of virtues that the Rev. Messick credited to Albert was his ability to always show respect for others. From the smallest child who wanted to fiddle, to sewing a dress to bring his wife to wear home from the hospital with her first baby, Albert paid attention to the needs and rights of others he encountered.

Walt described it this way, "Someone said last night, 'If everyone lived like Albert did, this would be a much better world for all of us to live in.' How true. He respected others and hoped for the same from them."

Albert understood intuitively and from his own experience how important music could be in someone's life and was always respectful when that need arose. Albert told one high school student interviewer, "I've had dozens of people come in here a wantin' a musical instrument, you know," he said. "You could look at them and tell they didn't have anything. And they'd tell you they had nothing to buy it with, but they'd sure like to have it. Well, I'd say, 'Take it on. You can pay me when you have the money.' You

Seven—The Last Leaf on the Tree

know I've only been beat out of one instrument like that. One instrument in all that I've sold and let 'em take away like that. I guess I might be a pretty good judge of character," said Albert.

He once recalled a storeowner, a man Albert called "preacher," telling him that he could always trust a customer who came in needing fatback and beans. "That man will pay for that. He would always pay his accounts and be honest with me," Albert recalled the man telling him, "but if he comes in and starts carrying all the cakes and honey out of here, he ain't gonna pay for that." That idea, that there was a basic decency in the heart of most men and women, was how Albert lived. He trusted folks to show basic human dignity, and in return, they trusted him.

Albert learned to respect others and their delicate needs when he was young and never forgot the importance of it. "When we were young," he recalled, "we looked out for each other. And I think that's the way the world should be today, too. I think if people looked out for each other now, the world would be a much happier and better place to live in. I've tried to practice that all up through the years." That respect for other people was at the core of Albert's Appalachian upbringing and resonated throughout his life. It is the engine that drives a true Appalachian spirit.[8]

Music

Walt identified Albert's intense love of and appreciation for music as one of the most powerful chapters in his life. "How many people do you know who couldn't wait to get to work because they loved what they were doing so much? He loved to make music but got more satisfaction from building fiddles for others. His day often began at 6:00 a.m. in his shop. He was so dedicated to the preservation of old-time music that he spent countless hours and days with others to encourage their interest."

Songs that Albert loved to play, like "Hangman's Reel," "Old Sport," and "Nancy Blevins," are played all over the world in Albert's memory and honor, around remote campfires at old-time gatherings and in concert halls in the hearts of our greatest cities. Albert's recordings live on with the recent release of two volumes of his fiddling put together by his nephew, Kilby Spencer, among others, and distributed by the Field Recorders Collective.

From the moment that his neighbor, Corbett Stamper, first played a few fiddle tunes for a young Albert Hash on that rainy day, to the sounds of the notes on the first fiddle he ever built, to sitting alone with his great uncle, George Finley, as he passed down to Albert the ancient Appalachian sounds of his forefathers, Albert resonated with the music of his beloved Blue Ridge. He resonated vibrations that were felt in the lives of countless men and women, who, like Wayne Henderson, found great joy and worth in building musical instruments.

His resonance flowed into the fingers of hundreds upon hundreds of young fiddlers like Brian Grim of the Konnarock Critters who heard him play and spent hours learning from him in person or from listening to his records, note for note. And Albert resonated with his many devoted fans who, to this day, nearly 40 years after his death, follow the Whitetop Mountain Band that he founded from concert to concert to dance and listen to his music, the music of Grayson County.

Children

The Rev. Messick felt that a special chapter in the book of Albert Hash would be reserved for his love of children. "Last night and today is a tribute to what children meant to him," Walt said. "For those of you who have taken lessons at the firehouse or been there to observe know that he loved children and was eager to share with them his love and talents. And part of his love and talent was given to at least one young man who had no fiddle and Albert helped him build one of his own."

Starting with young Wayne Henderson and continuing throughout his adult live, Albert took great joy in seeing young people become passionate about playing music and making the instruments to do so. From leaving tools in young people's mailboxes, to giving fiddles to those who wanted to play, and tirelessly giving lessons to young people who traveled from far and wide to learn the Whitetop Mountain style, Albert's life was that of a true teacher, one who gives selflessly so that others might share in the joy of music.

"Albert knew how to manage children, and he could get the best from them," declared principal Wilma Testerman, who had helped Albert start the music program at the firehouse. "He hadn't had any training, but he always expected the best and they gave it to him." The children in the Mt. Rogers program not only learned to play their instruments and to play in a string band, but many of them learned to make their own instruments from Albert and Audrey. During the first year of the program, one of the

Seven—The Last Leaf on the Tree

Albert playing for two of his granddaughters, 1978. The one beside him is Amanda Miller Coldiron (Audrey's youngest) and the other is Elizabeth Miller Sizemore (Audrey's oldest) (photograph by Mark Sanderford).

students, under their tutelage, made a fiddle and presented it to the superintendent of the school district, ensuring the future of the program.[9]

"He had a knack for it," his daughter Audrey said. "He'd talk to them, and he'd let them know that he expected them to learn and to play. The kids were there because they wanted to be, they chose to be there and they chose to learn what Albert taught them. He was so proud of them when they got it, and so patient when they didn't."[10]

One of his granddaughters, Carla Osborne, remembered him as the "grandpa who always had time for you." No matter how big the crowds at his house, and no matter how many kids were underfoot, if you could get Albert's attention, Carla recalled, he would be totally with you. "One time when I was five, I had a loose tooth. I ran all over the house, showing it to family and visitors alike," Carla recalled. "Finally, Granny told me to go down to Granddaddy's shop and show him. He was real busy, but he stopped everything and said, 'Let me see that.' And then real gently, and precisely, he pulled it out. I didn't feel a thing. He had a way of making each of us feel like his favorite grandchild."[11]

Brian Grim, who with his sister Debbie took lessons at the firehouse, remembers being astonished at his teachers. "Not only would they teach us, they would jam with us after every lesson, with all of the students. There I was, just learning and I was playing the tune I just learned in a jam with Albert Hash and Thornton and Emily Spencer! It was so much fun," Brian remembered.

Debbie Grim Yates remembered his special way of dealing with children. "He was always very calm and grinned all the time. He was what I thought of as jolly," Debbie said. "He would have us playing with him at the school, performing at games and such, it made us feel so special. Everyone who learned from him learned well, because he was so kind and caring."[12]

Some of the students that Albert taught, like Brian and Debbie, became full-time musicians. Others went on to become instrument makers. Most, however, simply enriched their own lives and the lives of their families and their communities by sharing the music of the mountains that had been instilled in them by Albert Hash.

Realness

Walt declared another facet of Albert's life to be the simple fact that he was always real. "Albert was Albert," recalled Walt. "He wasn't phony. He didn't put on airs. The man we knew and loved *was* the man we loved and knew. That is a very rare quality to be found in a person these days."

Whether he was meeting a governor of Virginia or simply taking a chair around the stove at the Spencers' store, Albert was himself. His sense of humor, his keen ability to tell a story, and his strong sense of self that fostered his extreme humility by all accounts allowed Albert to rarely feel uncomfortable or to act pretentious in any group of people. He understood who he was and humbly gave of his talents as he could, purposely making friends along the way.

"He just made other people feel at ease," recalled Jerry Smith. "He was just Albert, whoever he was with, and that allowed everyone else to be themselves."

Musician and radio host Paul Brown has a powerful memory of Albert that captures his realness. "I was at the fiddler's convention at Fries, Virginia," recalls Paul, "and I hadn't gotten to speak with Albert that time. But I just remember watching him. He stopped to talk to someone who was nearby. Someone had gotten his attention as he was walking towards the stage. It was one of those moments that became etched into my memory. He stopped to talk to this person for a moment. He looked at this person, only for a second, but the warmth of the smile that he had on his face, I've never forgotten," recalled Paul. "And I remember thinking, right then, 'That is the essence of Albert Hash.'"

"He just had this delightful smile on his face as he talked and he inclined his head to really listen to that person," Paul continued, "and to make him feel welcome. It was one of those body language things. It was just one of those momentary things, but it said it all. And I thought, 'This is the reason that people really like this man, it is so apparent.' He was a genuinely warm, caring, decent person, and I never forgot that moment."

It was just that realness, that ability to engage with anyone and draw him out, to see his potential and not his failings, that nearly everyone who knew him can recall about Albert Hash.

A Valuable Life

Finally, Walt closed the recounting of Albert's life by assuring the gathering that Albert's life was short but not in vain. "The last chapter is the ultimate and triumphant conclusion to his story. Albert's life was not in vain. His life was not wasted. It was shorter than any of us wished. I keep saying if only he could have lived five more years. But he accomplished so much in his 64 years. We are living testimonies to it. His instruments and other works will survive and live on indefinitely. Our memories of him are packed with images, stories and events for future recalling and enjoyment. And hopefully our lives are different because of our crossing paths with his."

The Rev. Messick opined that now that Albert was free from earthly binds he could "finally make that perfect fiddle that he was always one step away from here on earth."

The real value of Albert's life can be measured in the legacy he left behind, in the continuation of the work he did to preserve and proudly present the Appalachian music and the culture of the Blue Ridge to the rest of the world that is carried on by those he taught and those his life and work continue to influence.

A small crowd huddled together around the gravesite, just down the mountain from Albert's home on Cabin Creek, in Haw Orchard, just up the road from Thornton and Emily's home. Walt, his coat buttoned tight against the cold, read a brief scripture and said a prayer of committal—"ashes to ashes, dust to dust." People lingered as the casket was lowered into the grave, wiping tears from their eyes, still hearing those beautiful mountain melodies on the wind that blew across Haw Orchard Mountain. And as the line of cars and pick-ups drove slowly out of the cemetery, each mourner heading back to his or her separate life but bonded forever by their common love and respect for a great Appalachian man, the sun broke through the clouds, turning the day to gold.

Eight

The Legacy of Albert Hash

*"If the wind on Whitetop Mountain
sounds vaguely like fiddle music,
It's most likely the mountain's way of
paying tribute to a fine country gentleman"
—From the stone on Albert's grave
in Haw Orchard Cemetery*

A Legacy of Appalachian Values

There exists, in cyberspace, a documentary film, made in the ephemeral black and white style before talking pictures, entitled *Below Whitetop*. It was made by the Lutheran Church to celebrate its accomplishments in bringing "progress" to the highlanders of Grayson County, Virginia. In the fleeting first few frames that depict life in the isolated mountains, you see a young man, dressed in overalls, hair slicked back with kitchen grease, meticulously carving out a fiddle top with his whittling knife. It is Albert Hash. The irony of this image in lieu of Albert's long and meaningful legacy cannot be escaped.

While *Below Whitetop* attempts to depict the great need of the area in the late 1920s, for religious intervention, for a "training" school, for spiritual, educational, moral and technical guidance for the "mountain people," the life of one of the camera's fleeting subjects, Albert Hash, stands in direct defiance of the stereotypes that the film's producers put forth. Albert, like many of his neighbors and friends, lived and flourished through self-determination and self-reliance, through a fierce commitment to community, through kindness and generosity and by living true to the beliefs and the ways of their mountain culture, a culture that still shines deep in the Blue Ridge.

Appalachian Fiddler Albert Hash

While raised in abject poverty, mostly without a father at home, schooled in one- and two-room schools, and never having the opportunity to travel far from home or visit the great cities of the planet, Albert lived the life of a true artist, the life of a teacher, the life of a moral and decent father and neighbor and the life of a self-made and self reliant man. Albert readily embraced the descriptor "hillbilly" and demonstrated the real meaning of such a term—a human shaped by the best of what his geography, his history, his community and the legacies of others before him could teach him, not the stereotypical mountain life depicted in the media, or in David Vance's recent incrimination of Appalachian culture, *Hillbilly Elegy*, or in other wrongfully guided attempts to portray the "Appalachian attitude."[1]

Vance appears to blame the victims for what has become of some poor, misguided and bitter people in the South who have turned to drug abuse, violence, and self-hatred because of their impoverished lives and circumstances. Albert saw the changes in Appalachian people over time as a choice for some, as consequences of their abandoning the values of their heritage for money and the demands of a life in the mills and factories that did not exist in the mountains.

Albert's own legacy is like the creeks and streams that flow down from Whitetop and Mt. Rogers, shaped by the mountains and yet doing much shaping of its own. As the years since his death have flowed on, his influence on old-time mountain music and on Appalachian fiddle making appear to deepen and broaden. If a legacy is measured by the transference of one's gifts to future generations, then the legacy of Albert Hash has just begun.

What Albert brought to the people of his area of Appalachia was a pride that cannot be constructed or bought. His life gave testimony to the value of their musical and cultural heritage. It provided living proof that "the Appalachian way" is one of relying on yourself to better the lives of your family, your friends, and your neighbors (both your geographic and your cultural neighbors). It was not one of retreat, bitterness and ignorance that is often portrayed as the Appalachian lifestyle.

Once the passion for old-time music was born in him, he did not see lack of money or resources as obstacles. He dreamed of building a fiddle on which to play mountain songs and then he did it. He taught himself to find the notes on the fingerboards to produce the melodies he loved and then he sought out his elders to make sure he learned it right. Poverty, lack of resources, isolation, lack of formal training, these were

Eight—The Legacy of Albert Hash

merely small impediments to be worked around, not fatalities in Albert's life.

The changes that Albert had seen in the mountains over the years of his life did worry him, however. He wasn't worried about who the mountain people were, but who they had become. "They have drastically changed, most of them," Albert sadly reminisced. "Most of them have abandoned their little farms and the good life here, and gone down off of the mountain and went into a factory somewhere. They've wrecked their nerves and they've breathed the pollution of those mills and factories," he said.[2]

His vision of what they lost was clear. "They left the real good life, the wholesome life of it, for the money. Actually, I would rather see the mountains back like it used to be. Now the depression days was bad days you know, but I would like to see it where a man could tie a few chicken legs together and throw 'em over his shoulder and take 'em to the store and buy his clothing, and take his eggs to the store and sell them, and raise his green beans and sell them and so on. What the heck's the difference? You just lived then and you just live now. And what you had then, you appreciated so much more than what you have now," Albert said.

He felt they had forgotten the very premise of mountain life. "And another thing, you didn't have to jump up to an alarm clock," he went on. "People didn't have to roll out of bed way before daylight to get somewhere. They worked a reasonable day's work, they visited, they stayed all night with each other, they went to see each other and life was easier. It was much simpler. A man had all day to make a pair of drawbars and a fence if he wanted to. These days no one has any time. You live to an alarm clock."

This was how Albert lived the best days of his life in the mountains. Teaching music, building fiddles that could sing, growing a garden, tending to his clocks, visiting with his and Ethel's many friends, and having time to devote to the beauty of his beloved mountains. When he could choose, that was how Albert would use his time. He loved watching his daughters and their families grow and having time to win many a festival and tell many a yarn. And as it turns out, that way of life, the mountain way, Albert's way, is carried on by many of the people he influenced and is being passed down to yet another generation. The last leaf on the tree, in his demise, has helped a number of buds on the tree of Appalachian culture.

In the 1970s, Loyal Jones, from the Appalachian Studies Department at Berea College in Kentucky, wrote a vital and powerful tome in a magazine simply titled "Appalachian Values." It was later published as a beautiful book. Jones could have been writing about Albert Hash as he laid out 10 essential traits of true Appalachian culture.[3]

One of the most important values of the real Appalachian, Jones noted, was the Appalachian *sense of humor*. Albert loved a good joke, especially on himself, from mimicking the call of a bull to displaying a sign in his workplace "Albert Hash, Rectomologist." Nearly everyone who knew Albert loved him for his quick wit and his ability to play a practical joke. His legacy of humor is recounted around woodstoves in the high mountains.

The qualities of *independence, self-reliance* and *pride* are among Albert's strongest legacies. As a child in the mountains he dreamed of making fiddles and then he did so. Later he dreamed of making clocks and made grand ones, some with all wood parts. The mountains themselves taught him and his brothers self-reliance and that sometimes self-reliance means having to share hand-me-downs, chores, and even jobs. Albert was not alienated because of independence and self-reliance; he was brought closer to his family, friends and community and admired for those attributes. That legacy was passed on to his torchbearers.

Neighborliness and *hospitality* were constant themes in Albert and Ethel's way of life and continue to be in the lives of those who have followed in their path. If Albert had a skill, he would share it. If he knew a great tune, he'd play it for you. If your church or school needed a good band to play for your dance, or corn shuckin' or bean stringin', he would be there, fiddle in hand. Sharing and giving to his neighbors is maybe Albert's greatest legacy and it is being carried on by many of the musicians, luthiers and neighbors who knew him. He welcomed hundreds of young strangers into his home and into his work. Now those hundreds are carrying on his work.

Loyal Jones saw *familism* as central to Appalachian values. Albert Hash saw it as a lifelong commitment. The only time he left Appalachia for any length of time was to accompany his brothers to alternative service during World War II. He was rooted in his family, making sure that his brother-in-law learned the music, caring for his mother after she wore out, teaching his daughters and their sons and daughters the mountain ways and his love of all things Appalachia. To Albert, family came first, but so many of his neighbors acted like they were family because his love and compassion for them made them feel that way. This legacy continues

Eight—The Legacy of Albert Hash

with the Spencer family, his cousin Dean Sturgill's family, and with Wayne Henderson's family as well as his grandchildren's families. Like Albert, these folks hold their family close and put them first. Their friends are as family.

One of the most powerful Appalachian values that Albert possessed was *personalism*. Albert went to great lengths to avoid offending other people, especially those he was teaching to play or coaching in making fiddles. One of his favorite phrases, according to Thornton Spencer, was "I believe he can learn that thing." He used variations of that phrase on Thornton when he was learning fiddle, on Flurry Dowe who wanted desperately to play the banjo, and on Wayne Henderson wanting to build a playable guitar. He was optimistic about people, trying to always measure their potential rather than their weaknesses, even to the point of sometimes having to use band money to get them out of jail. "It was just the way he looked at you, you knew he was there for you, all there," said Paul Brown.

Albert's *sense of beauty* was evident in the intricate carvings, from peacocks to parrots, from damsels to witches, that adorned his fiddles. They seemed to have lives of their own. He also appreciated the beauty that lay at the heart of the melody in an old-time fiddle tune. He would celebrate that melody in a clear, concise manner with his powerful bowing style, bringing forth unique rhythms within the melody.

People would be drawn to the stage when Albert played and his campground jams were often nearly trampled by those who wanted to see who was playing so beautifully. Fiddlers young and old craved Albert's sense of beauty.

Albert told an interview from England, "I'd rather be in these mountains than just about anywhere else in the world." His *love of place* was shown in nearly everything he did, from promoting local music to carving figures featuring the creatures that inhabited his mountain life. He had spent time away from the mountains, but he much preferred to be at home, deep in the Grayson highlands. His love was always reflected in his performances when he would tell an audience, "This is the way we do it back home." Always, the audiences who loved him nearly as much as he loved his mountains would applaud with laughter.

Albert was never known to preach or tell others what they should think or believe. His *religion* was one of action. He was known in the mountain communities in which he lived and traveled as the person who could be called upon to help solve problems. His religion required him to give of himself, of his talents, of his larger-than-life personality and of his humble spirit to those less fortunate. If he saw a young person who wanted to learn, who wanted to better himself or herself at something, he religiously poured his heart and soul into helping that person fulfill their passion. He did this for his own daughters.

The Torch Bearer: Audrey Hash Ham

Audrey took her father's death hard. For many of the adult years of her life, her dad had been her daily inspiration, her guiding light. He had taught her the ways of a crafts maker, the intricacies of woodworking and of wood's ability to magically transfer sounds from the mind of one person to the ear of another. She had learned to bend, shape, join, and shave wood into instruments that were as beautiful to behold as they were to listen to. That was her father's gift to her and she respected it.

She was 34 when her father passed and she used the grief of his loss to accelerate her advocacy for mountain culture and mountain music. She had written grants to start and continue her and her father's work at the fire station and with Emily Spencer's help had solidified the music program at Mt. Rogers School. Thanks to their work, hundreds of mountain musicians have sprouted and enriched the lives of their families, their neighbors and their communities across southwest Virginia.

Her first order of business

Albert's younger daughter, Audrey Hash (Hamm) ca. 1980, photograph copyright Sylvia Picher, used by permission.

Eight—The Legacy of Albert Hash

was to finish, to the best of her abilities in her grief, the orders that were on her father's workbench. Meticulously, sometimes with tears in her eyes, she finished the carvings and intricate designs that Albert had begun. When that was done, she returned to the dulcimer and fiddle orders that kept pouring into the shop. Eventually, she moved the shop out of her mother's basement and built a new shop outside her home in Mouth of Wilson. While raising her two daughters, she carried on the family's work, with one exception. Although she was a fine musician in her own right, she rarely played out. Instead she taught others to play and build instruments with a deep understanding of her father's work. Although she had been featured as a ballad singer earlier in her life and could play the fiddle and dulcimer well, she rarely shared those talents other than to test and demonstrate her instruments.

"It's all I've ever known," Audrey told David Holt in an interview for his PBS series *Folkways*. "My first memory is standing at the window watchin' my father build a fiddle, and I can well remember thinking, 'Wow, how can you take a board and make something that beautiful?'" When asked by Holt if she built fiddles differently than her father had, she replied, "Oh, there are small, tiny differences but not enough to change the tone of the instrument."

Audrey had learned a powerful lesson from her father that was at the very essence of her instrument building, she told David Holt. This lesson seems to encapsulate Albert's teaching in one short sentence. "You've got to put the love into that instrument, in order to make that instrument something that someone will treasure," she said.[4]

Joined in her shop by Archie Powers, who had learned from her father, and his son Carl, Audrey labored over the next 30 years to build beautiful fiddles in her dad's style, some selling for as much as $15,000 and others being purchased to be featured at the Smithsonian and museums across the world. Audrey, like her father, was humble the way the mountain culture required. "A fiddle is an educated guess," she said, "and I ain't got too much education."

Her dulcimers and fiddles are still highly in demand following her death in 2013 at the age of 64. Ironically, like her father's, Audrey's life was cut short largely due to cigarette smoking. She was still taking orders that two of her students, Chris Testerman and Jackson Cunningham, both local young men though Jackson originally hails from southern Oregon, who had met Audrey in the Mt. Rogers School program, helped finish. She had mentored these two young men and they quickly became her collaborators. Both Chris and Jackson continue the work Audrey started, building and teaching instruments and playing music in the Albert Hash tradition.

The Next Last Leaf: Thornton Spencer

It was not by accident that Thornton Spencer would become the next to echo the brilliant sounds of Albert's musical legacy. He honored his brother-in-law and dear friend by continuing the musical paths that Albert had hiked, and, in many ways, expanding on them. Thornton had been raised with the same values, beliefs and culture of the mountains and through Albert had developed an artistry of his own that echoed not only Albert's skill but also echoed many of his own forbearers and influences in old-time music.

Much like Albert, the hunger for the sound of native fiddle music rose in Thornton at a very young age and stayed with him until his death. Thornton spent much of his pre-adolescent and adolescent years with Albert, and he became his greatest champion and promoter while at the same time developing his own style and his own legacy. He was not an Al-

Thornton Spencer shortly before his 2017 death, sharing a story about his brother-in-law, Albert Hash (photograph by Jim Kacsmarik).

bert clone by any means; he was a mountaineer in the tradition of Albert Hash, or, as Albert might have put it, Thornton was "the next last leaf on the tree."

Thornton also had a careful ear and a skilled hand on the bow, and he listened and learned the native sounds of the mountain musicians that Albert introduced him to. No one more than Thornton understood the intricacies of the area's fiddle music and Albert's interpretation of it. He dedicated most of his life to making sure he had it right, and, much like his mentor, to unselfishly and skillfully teaching the style to anyone who wanted to learn from him.

Albert described, in 1975, Thornton's musical abilities. "Thornton's been playin' with me now since he was just about 12," Albert said. "He took interest in the guitar at first and he plays a guitar real well. In fact, I'd say Thornton is one of the better hands to back up a fiddle there is. He hits the good old Riley Puckett chords and a few of his runs. But fiddle is his main instrument. I took a great interest in helpin' him learn these old tunes and I mighta' done too good! He's been beatin' me at theses fiddling conventions now. We just take it about 'whippety cut' on whose gonna win, but usually one of us comes in first and the other second."[5]

Thornton's early influences included not only Albert but also locals like Jont Blevins (who played both banjo and fiddle), Corbett Stamper, who had first piqued Albert's interest in the fiddle, his distant cousin Ola Belle Reed, who was born in the area and often returned, and from the playing of Munsey Gaultney, Otis Burris and Joe Sheets, among many others. No one, according to Kevin Donleavy, in his definitive narrative of southwestern Virginia and northwestern North Carolina musicians called *Strings of Life*, knew more about the genealogy of the area's music than Thornton Spencer.[6]

Not long after Albert's passing, Thornton and Emily began carrying on the work of the Whitetop Mountain Band, playing a grueling schedule of festivals, dances and concerts. The year Albert passed, 1983, the band returned to Bobby Patterson's Heritage Records studio and recorded their fourth record, *Winebarger's Mill*. In homage to Albert, they included, posthumously, five cuts that had been previously recorded with Albert and Thornton twin fiddling and Flurry Dowe on banjo. The other cuts, with only Thornton fiddling, are strong and true to the tradition, showing that the band would not only survive but thrive with Thornton taking the lead.

Musician Andy Cohen, who wrote the liner notes for the *Winebarg-*

er's Mill recording, called Thornton's fiddling "a study in precision and smoothness." He went on to state that "he has a sharp ear for musical subtleties and a passion for learning about other musicians' techniques. He has become one of the foremost musicians in the Southern mountains."

In the new configuration Emily Spencer was strong and driving on clawhammer banjo with Tom Barr on bass. Some cuts featured a strong rhythm with two guitars played by Becky Haga and Fred Taylor. This new sound seemed to propel the mountain dancers, who flocked to the band's performances, into a mad furry.

The Whitetop Mountain Band, like all of Albert's bands, had always been primarily a dance band, with some ballads and novelty songs thrown in for concerts. However, the new configuration, piloted by Thornton and backed by Emily's driving style of clawhammer, drew dancers by the hundreds. The band quickly drew a huge following both in Virginia and North Carolina and became favorites at the bigger conventions like Galax and festivals MerleFest, which had been started to honor Doc Watson's son. Venues that employed the services of the Whitetop Band were almost guaranteed a large turnout if they provided a plywood floor for flatfoot dancing.

In 1992, Tom and Becky Barr left the band and Tom began to devote his time to making fiddles in the manner that Albert had taught him and to running a popular musical instrument store in Galax. Thornton and Emily continued to carry on, adding Johnny and Nancy Gentry to the band line-up on guitar and bass. The band continued to be in constant demand throughout the region and beyond, as Thornton continued to carry the torch lit by his older brother-in-law. In 1982, Thornton and Emily's first child was born, Kilby Albert Spencer. A few years later, another child, Martha, was born. By the mid–'90s, both children began dancing and playing on stage with the band, both having demonstrated unusual gifts for interpreting old-time mountain music.

In recent years, both Kilby and Martha have become stars of old-time music in their own rights, while at the same time continuing to "come home" to play with their mother and father in the Whitetop Mountain Band. Kilby played guitar and fiddle and other instruments with a variety of bands, including forming, with his sister, the band Spencer Branch, and spearheading the Crooked Road Ramblers, one of the region's most popular old-time bands. The Ramblers continue to be a popular dance band, playing many of the venues that the Whitetop Mountain Band have played, but also appealing to younger members of the old-time music community.

Eight—The Legacy of Albert Hash

Kilby, like his father and his uncle Albert, who he didn't get to know, has become a teacher of old-time fiddle. In possibly the greatest tribute to his uncle Albert, Kilby assisted the Field Recorders Collective, a not-for-profit label that publishes rare and out-of-circulation recordings of old-time musicians, to release two volumes of Albert's recordings. Kilby also honors his father's and Albert's legacy by collecting, collating and distributing rare recordings of old-time musicians from around the country. He is known as a collector's collector.

Martha, who learned to play clawhammer banjo from her mother as well as many of the old-time musicians in the Whitetop region, is also known for her dancing, fiddling, bass playing, guitar playing, and her ability to sing not only the old mountain ballads but also her own songs. A recent CD of hers got favorable reviews not only in the usual old-time and alt-country press but also in those far from the mountain, like *Rolling Stone*. She has toured Europe often and travels the country with her own band. For several years she has also been playing bass, dancing and thrilling audiences as part of a duo with famed mountain banjo player and singer Larry Sigmon. Sigmon and Barbara Poole started the duo, aptly called "The Unique Sound of the Mountains," in the late 1980s, and after Barbara's death in 2008, Martha took on the bass. The two are still called "The Unique Sound of the Mountains." In addition, she plays with several other bands including her own Martha Spencer Band and hosts a popular radio show on Radio Bristol that highlights her knowledge of old-time music.

The Whitetop Mountain Band continued to fulfill its role as one of the preeminent old-time bands in the country under Emily and Thornton's guidance until 2017, when at the age of 82, Thornton laid down his fiddle and was buried in Haw Orchard Cemetery, a few feet from his beloved brother-in law, Albert Hash. He had faithfully carried on Albert's legacy for well over 30 years past Albert's death. Included in his volume of work were eight more commercial recordings, culminating in *Things I Left Behind*, recorded shortly before his death.

Thornton never forgot the gift that Albert had given him. To symbolize that gift, for most of his fiddling years, he was seen performing in a black bowler hat that was given to him by Albert, a small but fitting tribute to his teacher and brother in-law.

Thornton as well as Emily had also recorded on many other musicians' albums and compilations, performed for governors and royalty, toured most of the United States as well as Australia and the British Isles, and appeared at the Smithsonian, the National Folklife Festival, the World Music Institute in New York, and countless festivals, campuses and venues including the beloved Carter Family Fold on many occasions. Thornton Spencer, like Albert, had also taught hundreds of people, young and old, how to play the music of the mountains that he loved so dearly. His later life carried on the traditions of the mountains that Albert had adhered to, and for his devotion to such a life he was adored.

The Teacher: Emily Spencer

Albert's legacy of teaching old-time music has been most embodied by the continuing work of his sister-in-law, Emily Spencer. From the founding of the program at Mt. Rogers School in 1982 to the present time, Emily has formally and informally taught mountain music in school programs, community college classes, and workshops, festivals, and old-time gatherings across the nation. Emily formalized the program that she, Thornton, Albert and Audrey began at the fire station and brought it into the schoolhouse.

Emily Paxton Spencer, musician and teacher, November 2017 (photograph by Jim Kacsmarik).

Eight—The Legacy of Albert Hash

Shortly after Albert's death, she organized a group of Mt. Rogers students into the Albert Hash Memorial Band. It became wildly popular and traveled as far as Florida and even marched in the Rose Bowl Parade, the first Appalachian string band to do so. Emily's work in this area, unselfishness and generosity are a great tribute to not only her skill as a musician and educator but also her commitment to the spirit of the mountains.

Along with Thornton, Emily continued to formally teach students at such prestigious music schools as the Swannanoa Gathering in Asheville, North Carolina; the Mountain Music School in Big Stone Gap, Virginia; the Cowan Creek Music School in Whitesburg, Kentucky; and the Floyd Old Time Gathering in Floyd, Virginia; and many others. Many full-time performers of old-time and bluegrass music owe their abilities to "Ms. Emily," as they often call her, the serious student of Appalachian culture who found her way to the mountains of southwest Virginia and has never left.

Thornton and Emily Spencer of the Whitetop Mountain Band playing a tune in their living room in Haw Orchard, Virginia. Thornton is wearing the bowler hat that Albert gave him (photograph by Jim Kacsmarik, 2017).

Following Thornton's death, many assumed that one formal legacy of Albert Hash, the Whitetop Mountain Band, would once and for all come to an end. However, it has evolved into what it was originally and continues to be—a family band. Now the band, under Emily's direction, is still seen regularly at dances in Galax, Mt. Airy, the Carter Family Fold, and the Floyd Country Store, with Kilby playing his father's tunes on an Albert Hash fiddle, Emily on banjo and vocals, Martha on guitar and vocals (and dancing!), and Debbie Bramer from nearby Fancy Gap, Virginia, on bass. In 2018, the female members of the band toured the British Isles with Martha playing fiddle. The Whitetop Mountain Band continues to be one of the most popular old-time acts in the nation.

The Memorial Festival

Emily and Thornton, with the help of many locals including Wayne Henderson, established in 1996 the Albert Hash Memorial Festival, held annually at Grayson Highlands State Park, just down the road a bit from Albert's Cabin Creek home and Haw Orchard Cemetery. Like a huge family reunion, musicians, neighbors, and those curious about Albert's legacy join for a day of music, dancing, story swapping and crafts in his honor. One of the highlights of the festival is a display of Albert Hash fiddles that often turn up from far and wide. Emily, with the support of many of Albert's friends, continues to oversee every aspect of the festival, ensuring it is in the tradition that Albert loved.

Although there are no contests, the festival features many of Albert's friends, younger musicians who may have learned from Albert or those who play in the Albert Hash tradition. On the day of the festival, attendees can see and hear many of Albert's fiddles played as well as some of the fiddle makers who learned the craft from Albert and carry on the tradition by bringing their work to the festival. The day always features a performance by Wayne Henderson exquisitely showcasing one of his hand-built guitars, playing it as only he can.

Legacy in Wood

No one seems to know just how many fiddles Albert Hash built in his lifetime. Estimates range from 50 to 800. As we researched this book,

Eight—The Legacy of Albert Hash

many people told us they had an Albert Hash fiddle, and many more knew of someone who did. Yet more had fiddles or dulcimers built by his daughter, Audrey, often made with Albert's loving oversight and co-signature. As you can imagine, those in circulation are highly coveted and rarely, if ever, turn up on the market.

Musician Matt Kinman was walking down the street in Nashville a few years ago with Albert's niece, Martha, when he spied what appeared to be an Albert Hash fiddle in a Nashville pawnshop. To his surprise, he went in and was able to buy it at a very reasonable price to give to Martha, who until then didn't have one of her uncle's fiddles.[7] Some of the

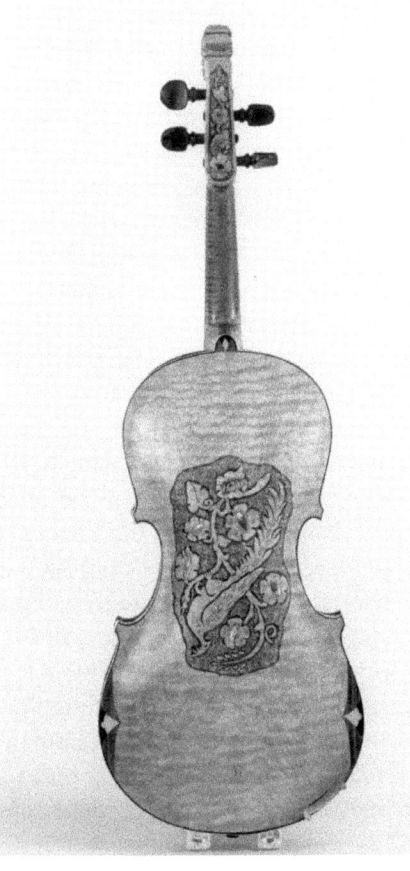

Front view of an Albert Hash fiddle (photograph by Mark Sanderford).

Back view of carving on an Albert Hash fiddle (photograph by Mark Sanderford).

unnumbered but often named fiddles have sold for thousands of dollars, but most rest peacefully in the music rooms of musicians across the country and the world, usually surrounded by the stories their owners willingly tell. They love to go on and on about their fiddles and about Albert Hash and how they came to own one of his fiddles.

Much greater than the legacy of the actual fiddles he built is the knowledge and passion for instrument building that Albert passed on. Audrey built fiddles for 40 years. Wayne Henderson has built more than 800 guitars, many while using one of Albert's pocketknives and a replicating machine that Albert designed. In true Albert fashion, Wayne teaches a large batch of young luthiers, many of whom are successful instrument makers, including Jayne, his own daughter, who builds ukuleles and mandolins in her dad's shop.

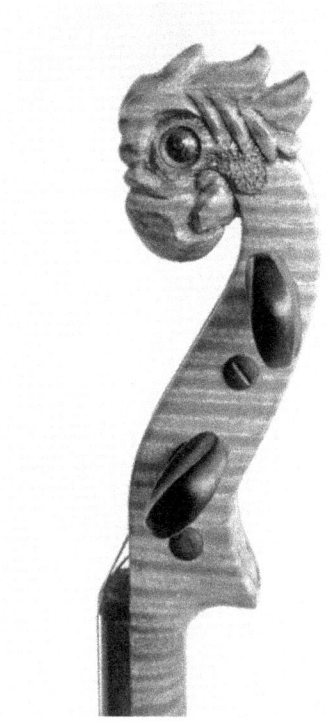

Carved headstock of an Albert Hash fiddle (photograph by Mark Sanderford).

Walter Messick, the former minister who preached Albert's funeral service, has built more than 1000 dulcimers on Cabin Creek thanks to Albert and Audrey's apprenticeship of him. Even though he still can't really play a mountain dulcimer, others play his dulcimers across the world—an irony that would not have been lost on Albert.

Tom Barr is still building fiddles in the style he learned from Albert and sells them at his fiddle shop in Galax, Virginia. Randall Eller, who visited Albert with his brother on a rainy day more than 30 years ago and left with a mission to build fiddles, continues to build Hash-style fiddles and mandolins in his Chilhowie, Virginia, shop.

On and on the tradition goes. Jack Branch of Bristol, Virginia, recently passed away after 35 years of building fiddles in the style he learned by apprenticing with Albert when he was injured and had to change careers. His instruments are played in orchestras across the country. Archie Elmer Powers and his son, Carl, both learned to make instruments as young men from Albert. Elmer made many fiddles for family and friends until his death in 2016.

Among the frequent visitors to Albert's shop in the 1970s was a young man named Joe Thrift. Joe, who was at the time apprenticing in guitar- and banjo-building with Dave Sturgill, another person Albert had encouraged, wanted to learn to build fiddles. Albert encouraged him so much, in fact, that a few months later he left for violin building school in England for nearly three years. When he returned, he not only continued to build fiddles as Albert encouraged him but also became a legendary musician, co-founding the alt-country group Donna the Buffalo and the high-energy old-time band The Red Hots. Joe now teaches sold-out fiddle-building classes at Surry Community College and is launching a whole new generation of fiddle makers.[8]

Chris Testerman currently has a shop near Whitetop where he builds fiddles in the style he learned from Audrey, having grown up learning to play and building his first fiddle in the traditional music classes started by Albert and carried on by Audrey, Thornton and Emily.[9] Thus, the last leaf on the tree, long after its fall to the earth, continues to fertilize many roots and branches throughout southwest Virginia.

The Last Leaf

There are small monuments to Albert Hash throughout his Blue Ridge Mountains and beyond. The visitors' center at Grayson Highlands State Park near his Cabin Creek home proudly displays one of his fiddles directly across from one of Wayne Henderson's guitars. The Smithsonian Institution in Washington houses several of his fiddles and many of his original recordings captured by traveling folklorists. His recordings are popular purchases from the Field Recorders Collective and there is talk of a third volume or a tribute recording. Heartwood, the southwest Virginia artists' collective that houses the headquarters of Virginia's Crooked Road Music Trail, can trace almost all of their luthiers' skills back to either Audrey or Albert Hash. Starting with Wayne Henderson, Albert consciously recruited mountain people to build mountain instruments.

Anyone who travels on the Crooked Road will find a small memorial to Albert in Grayson County outside the local gas station in Whitetop.

There are small exhibits dedicated to him and the Whitetop Band at the Blue Ridge Music Center on the Blue Ridge Parkway and in the Museum of Ashe County History in Jefferson, North Carolina. You can hardly attend a local jam session in southwest Virginia or northwestern North Carolina without someone mentioning his name as they start "Hangman's Reel," "Nancy Blevins" or "Old Sport," or any fiddle tunes that have come to represent his playing.

The deepest impact that Albert Hash may have created may have not come from his musical ability, and it may not have come from his ability to take a block of wood and to "whittle away everything that isn't a fiddle," as he often said. Albert's most important legacy may not even be the gifts of music and woodwork he gave his students. In the end, Albert's greatest legacy may be the manner in which he lived his life, the legacy of a simple mountain man who lived true to the ideals he was raised with in the Blue Ridge—simplicity, commitment, resourcefulness, kindness, respect, caring, community and tradition. All of these life ingredients were sprinkled with an essential light coating of humor.

Musician, folklorist, and radio personality Paul Brown remembers sitting in a small campsite with Albert and several other old-time musicians when, out of the blue, Albert began to reveal that sometimes, when he was on one of his many walks through the mountains, he would, when no one else was around and he came upon an electric fence, just stop and put both of his hands on it and hold on. "I just like it," said Albert. "It makes me feel jazzed."

Paul and the other musicians laughed, nervously, assuming this was another of Albert's never-ending jokes. "There was something in his eyes," Paul remembered, "that made me know he was serious, that he really did this." In many ways this was pure Albert Hash. He was a man who could find pleasure in what most people and animals found unpleasant, a brief encounter with an electric fence. He lived life to the minute, and he loved to "feel jazzed."

Here was a man who as a child knew that his family couldn't afford the luxury of a fiddle for him to learn on, so at the age of nine built one on his own. Here, also, was a man who remembered the hunger he felt for that fiddle as well as the pride he felt when he was able to fill that hunger on his own. So, for the next 50 years, he unselfishly showed others how to feed their own musical needs.

Albert Hash was a man raised in poverty who knew that he sometimes had to depend on his mother and brothers or the help and kindness

Eight—The Legacy of Albert Hash

of their neighbors to have clothes and food, find work, share music, learn skills and live in a community. He practiced that sharing of material things and of intangibles every day of his life. He gave freely of his knowledge and his tools, of his well-honed mountain wisdom, to all those who would listen.

Albert Hash was a man who knew that without tradition, without a sense of place and the historical and cultural parts that were attached to that place, one was in danger of becoming lost in a world that has in some ways failed to invade and take away the uniqueness of upper Grayson County. The world of huge box stores and fast food frenzies, the world where art and music is just a mass-produced commodity, the world where nearly everyone talks, dresses, acts and lives the same life. He lived not in fear of that encroachment into the mountains, but in defiance of it.

He could easily travel to town to work to help mass produce electrical parts that would be used to modernize homes across the world and then go home to a house with no electricity and running water. In that house he would play music that had roots in other centuries on instruments he had built with his own hands. He valued and enjoyed that dichotomy that was his life because it stayed true to his Appalachian roots.

The life of Albert Hash gives us a special vision of what we may well be in danger of losing in the Appalachians and in the nation. It gives us a glimpse into the great men and women who settled this nation and developed its hope and ideals, the Americans who painfully built cities out of wilderness while carrying on, in their lives, the traditions, ideals and customs

One of the fiddles that Albert built to put on display at the Knoxville World's Fair.

of their own heritage, of their own tribes. These men and women built a civilized society that honored its roots by preserving and passing on the diverse traditions from which it was grounded. While some say Appalachian people are slow to change, many of them lead quiet, proud lives born out of a cultural tradition of kindness, caring and simplicity.

Much like the last leaf on the tree that falls to the ground each late fall, giving in its death unselfishly of its very being to become part of the compost, to fertilize the ground that nurtures the tree it came from, Albert's life, his music, his teachings and his fiddles will continue to feed our Appalachian culture for decades to come.

Appendix I
Discography: Albert Hash

Whitetop, Albert Hash and the Whitetop Mountain Boys, Mountain Records 311 (1976).

Cacklin' Hen, Albert Hash and the Whitetop Mountain Band, Mountain Records 313 (1977). Reissued in 1980, as Heritage Records 27.

Albert Hash and the Whitetop Mountain Band, Albert Hash and the Whitetop Mountain Band, Heritage Records 24 (1979).

Winebarger's Mill, Albert Hash and the Whitetop Mountain Band, Heritage Records (1983).

Albert Hash, Field Recorders Collective, FRC411 (2009).

Albert Hash, Volume 2, Field Recorders Collective, FRC707 (2015).

The Virginia Carolina Boys: Radio Shows 1966–1974, Museum of Ashe County History, Jefferson, North Carolina.

Compilations

The Art of Field Recording, Vol. 1, Dust to Digital Recordings, Disc 4, No. 9, "Omie Wise," and No. 10, "Train 45."

Old Originals, Vol. 2, Rounder Records (RR0058), B12, "Cripple Creek," and B13, "Nancy Blevins."

Appendix II
List of Known Recorded Tunes by Albert Hash (from Kilby Spencer)

Albert played a lot of tunes that unfortunately were never recorded. This list reflects only tunes that we have known recordings of.

Key of G

"Sally Goodin'"
"Cacklin' Hen"
"Rabbit Up a Gum Stump"
"Leather Britches"
"Did You Ever See the Devil, Uncle Joe?"
"Cumberland Gap"
"Lost John"
"Sally Ann"
"Little Brown Hand"
"Katy Hill"
"Flop-Eared Mule"
"Turkey in the Straw"
"Cripple Creek"
"Alabama Gals"
"Old Joe Clark"
"Drunk Man Blues"

"Baby-O"
"Ebenezer"
"Little Brown Jug"
"Omie Wise"
"Don't Go Out Tonight, My Darling"
"Handsome Molly"
"I've Always Been a Rambler"
"Lonely Tombs"
"The Great Physician"
"Honeysuckle Rose"
"Goodbye Booze"
"Love Letters in the Sand"
"Little Rosewood Casket"
"When the Snowflakes Fall Again"
"My Whitetop Mountain Home"

Key of D

"Arkansas Traveler"
"Old Molly Hare"
"Johnson Boys"
"Old Jimmy Sutton"
"Ragtime Annie"
"Liberty"
"Lost Indian"

"Black-Eyed Susie"
"Chicken Reel"
"Dry and Dusty"
"Soldier's Joy"
"Johnson's Old Grey Mule"
"Cricket on the Hearth"
"Forked Deer"

Appendix II

"Cindy"
"Sally Ann"
"Fly Around My Pretty Little Miss"
"Bonaparte's Retreat"

Key of A

"Bill Cheatham"
"Bile Them Cabbage Down"
"Pretty Little Indian"
"Grey Eagle"
"Sugarfoot Rag"
"Chitlin Cooking Time in Cheatham County"
"Cluck Old Hen" (AEAE tuning)
"Sourwood Mountain" (AEAE tuning)

"Nancy Blevins" (DADA tuning)
"Casey Jones" (DADA tuning)
"Old Time Cumberland Gap" (DADA tuning)

"Cripple Creek" (AEAE tuning)
"Train 45" (AEAE tuning)
"Hangman's Reel" (AEAE tuning)
"Old Sport" (AEAE tuning)
"Old Molly Hare" (AEAE tuning)
"Sally Goodin" (AEAE tuning)
"Old Joe Clark" (AEAE tuning)
"Black Mountain Rag" (AEAC# tuning)
"Walls of Jericho" (AEAC# tuning)

Key of C

"Billy in the Lowground"

Chapter Notes

Chapter One

1. David E. Whisnant, *All That Is Native and Fine* (Chapel Hill: University of North Carolina Press, 1984). Vivid description and some criticism of the three Whitetop Mountain festivals, is contained in this book and our re-creation is largely from this source.

2. Thornton Spencer, interview conducted by authors in his home, Haw Orchard, VA, October 2016.

3. Douglas Ogle, *Whitetop: The Great Meadow Mountain of Virginia* (Saltville, VA, 2011).

4. This tale circulates wildly in the area, but was noted by the State of Virginia on a sign describing the first survey of the area on the Virginia Creeper Trail. A state Rails to Trails project follows the old track bed of the steam rail built to haul timber off Whitetop.

5. Mason White, "Elliott, the Tragic Roosevelt," *Hudson Valley Review* 5, no. 1 (1988), 17–29.

6. Josh Beckworth, *Always Been a Rambler: G.B. Grayson and Henry Whitter, Country Music Pioneers of Southern Appalachia* (Jefferson, NC: McFarland, 2018).

7. Recounted in David Whisnant's account in note 1, from a personal interview with Albert Hash conducted by Whisnant.

8. Albert Hash, discussion of Uncle George Finley, *Albert Hash: Vol. 2* (from the collections of Wayne & Max Henderson, the Augusta Heritage Center, and the Spencer family), Field Recorders Collective CD 707, Track 2, 2015.

9. Paula H. Anderson-Green, *A Hotbed of Musicians: Traditional Music in the Upper New River Valley-Whitetop Region* (Knoxville: University of Tennessee Press, 2002).

10. Frank Weston's 1982 interview with Corbett Stamper as published on the liner notes of *Corbett Stamper*, Field Recorders Collective CD 306. Frank Weston, "Albert Hash: Fiddler and Fiddle Maker," *Old Time Music* 39 (1984), 12. This is a British publication.

11. This retelling of Albert's first fiddle is a compilation of three versions of the story: Albert Hash, personal interview with Edwin Lacy at Albert's Home, Cabin Creek, VA, 1977; Wayne Henderson, personal interview with authors, October 2016 (Wayne recounted this story as told to him by Albert); and Frank Weston, "Albert Hash: Fiddler and Fiddle Maker," *Old Time Music* 39 (1984), 12–13.

Chapter Two

1. Ronald D. Eller, *Miners, Millhands, and Mountaineers: Industrialization of the Appalachian South, 1880–1930* (Knoxville: University of Tennessee Press, 1982), 98.

2. Virginia Polytechnic Institute Agricultural Extension Services, *Rural Sociology Report* 64 (March 1948), retrieved August 30, 2018, https://www.newrivernotes.com/grayson_history_1940_housing_farm.htm.

3. Albert Hash, interview with Albert Hash, February 5, 1976, Appalachian State University Libraries Digital Collections, accessed September 6, 2017, http://omeka.library.appstate.edu/items/show/37314.

4. Sherree R. Tannen, *Kenneth Kill-*

Chapter Notes—Three

inger, *Mountain Missionary* (Lynchburg, VA: Warwick House, 1995), 5.

5. For an excellent discussion of the music in Grayson County during Albert's lifetime, see Kevin Donleavy's *Strings of Life: Conversations with Old-Time Musicians from Virginia and North Carolina* (Blacksburg, VA: Pocahontas Press, 2004).

6. A very brief video of Uncle Bud's dancing at the Whitetop festival can be viewed at *https://www.youtube.com/watch?v=NyFHtXdHzGc*.

7. The authors had brief but helpful phone discussions with Rhudy Hash, Jr., and Ernest Hash, Jr., Albert's nephews, and with Mary Ann Hash, Dennis Hash's daughter, from their homes near Appomattox, VA, and Trenton, NJ, in November 2018.

8. Frank Weston, "Albert Hash: Fiddler and Fiddle Maker," *Old Time Music* 39 (1984).

9. *Ibid.*

10. This was related to us by two sources: Thornton Spencer in an interview in his home in 2016 and Wayne Henderson in a personal interview in his shop in 2016.

11. Frank Weston, "Albert Hash: Fiddler and Fiddle Maker," *Old Time Music* 39 (1984).

12. Dean Sturgill, personal interviews with Dean at his home on Spencer Branch, NC, 2016, 2017, 2018. Dean was a first cousin to Albert's wife, Ethel, and lifelong friends with his cousin Thornton Spencer. He related accounts of Albert's pranks on three visits.

13. Albert Hash, interview with Albert Hash, February 5, 1976, Appalachian State University Libraries Digital Collections, accessed September 6, 2017, *http://omeka.library.appstate.edu/items/show/37314*.

14. *Ibid.*

15. *Ibid.*

16. *Ibid.*

17. Josh Beckworth, *Always Been a Rambler: G.B. Grayson and Henry Whitter, Country Music Pioneers of Southern Appalachia* (Jefferson, NC: McFarland, 2018); Charles K. Wolfe and Ted Olsen, eds., *The Bristol Sessions: Writings About the Big Bang of Country Music* (Jefferson, NC: McFarland, 2005).

18. Frank Weston, "Albert Hash: Fiddler and Fiddle Maker," *Old Time Music* 39 (1984).

19. *Ibid.*

20. Albert Hash, interview with Albert Hash, February 5, 1976, Appalachian State University Libraries Digital Collections, accessed September 6, 2017, *http://omeka.library.appstate.edu/items/show/37314*.

21. *Ibid.*

22. Frank Weston, "Albert Hash: Fiddler and Fiddle Maker," *Old Time Music* 39 (1984).

23. Kilby Spencer, who we interviewed in 2017, is Albert's nephew and Thornton Spencer's son. He is an authority on Albert's recordings and has amassed a collection of most of the known tapes and collections of Albert's playing. Kilby helped produce the Field Recorders Collective two-volume set of Albert's music.

24. This is from one of several letters between Albert and Ethel published online by Albert's niece, Martha Spencer. See *Mountain Music Magazine* (2015), accessed November 7, 2018, *https://mountainmusicmagazine.weebly.com/mountain-music-legacies*.

25. Frank Weston, "Albert Hash: Fiddler and Fiddle Maker," *Old Time Music* 39 (1984).

26. Audrey Hash Ham, interview with Martha Spencer, no date, accessed November 6, 2018, *https://www.youtube.com/watch?v=UZ0TDCUbrBk*.

27. Used with permission of the author, Dean Sturgill, see Field Recorders Collective 710, available online at *https://fieldrecorder.org/product/dean-sturgill-the-spencer-branch-fiddler-frc710/*.

28. Thornton Spencer, nterview conducted by the authors in his home, Haw Orchard, VA, October 2016.

29. Dean Sturgill, personal interviews with Dean at his home on Spencer Branch, NC, 2016, 2017, 2018.

30. *Ibid.*

31. Frank Weston, "Albert Hash: Fiddler and Fiddle Maker," *Old Time Music* 39 (1984).

Chapter Three

1. Jerry Smith, personal interview at Jerry's house in Jefferson, NC, 2017.

2. *Ibid.*
3. Albert Hash, interview with Albert Hash, February 5, 1976, Appalachian State University Libraries Digital Collections, accessed September 6, 2017, *http://omeka.library.appstate.edu/items/show/37314*.
4. We heard two very similar versions of the "I'll ask her tonight" story: Wayne Henderson, interview in Wayne's Rugby, VA, guitar shop in 2016, and Jerry Smith, personal interview at Jerry's house in Jefferson, NC, 2017.
5. *Ibid.* Note 3.
6. The entire discussion of clocks comes from the Appalachian State students' interview.
7. *Ibid.*
8. Albert Hash, interview with Edwin Lacy in his Cabin Creek home, 1979.
9. Jerry Smith, personal interview at Jerry's house in Jefferson, NC, 2017.
10. Thornton Spencer, "Fiddlin' Around in the Army," *Mountain Music Magazine* (2013), retrieved February 11, 2017, from *https://mountainmusicmagazine.weebly.com/the-haw-orchard-fiddler*.
11. Art Rosenbaum, phone interview, April 8, 2019.
12. Albert Hash, interview with Albert Hash, February 5, 1976, Appalachian State University Libraries Digital Collections, accessed September 6, 2017, *http://omeka.library.appstate.edu/items/show/37314*.
13. *Ibid.*
14. Albert Hash, interview with Edwin Lacy in his Cabin Creek home, 1979.
15. *Ibid.*

Chapter Four

1. Allen St. John, *Clapton's Guitar: Watching Wayne Henderson Build the Perfect Instrument* (New York: Free Press, 2005).
2. Wayne Henderson, interview in his guitar shop, November 12, 2016. Almost all of the material in this chapter, unless otherwise noted, came from two visits to Wayne Henderson's Rugby, VA, guitar shop in the summer of 2016. We interviewed Wayne twice and were given a very personal tour of many of the instruments he has collected over the years, including some Albert made. Proudly in his collection are two catalogues that were given to him by Albert on the day he went to him for help for building his first guitar.
3. Some of these recordings from the WKSK program of the Virginia Carolina Boys have been recently released on a CD available from the Museum of Ashe County History gift shop, with proceeds going to the museum.
4. Martin Fox, interview in the home of Wayne Erbsen, Asheville, NC, 2016.
5. Jerry Smith, personal interview at Jerry's house in Jefferson, NC, 2017.

Chapter Five

1. Mary Ellen Hash, phone interview from her home, November 2018. Mary is Albert's niece, daughter of Ernest Hash.
2. Dean Sturgill, personal interviews with Dean at his home on Spencer Branch, NC, 2016, 2017, 2018.
3. Flurry Dowe, interview with authors by Skype from his home, 2017.
4. Martin Fox, interview in the home of Wayne Erbsen, Asheville, NC, 2016.
5. Frank Weston, "Albert Hash: Fiddler and Fiddle Maker," *Old Time Music* 39 (1984).
6. *Ibid.*
7. *Ibid.* Wayne Henderson, interview in his guitar shop, November 12, 2016.
8. Frank Weston, "Albert Hash: Fiddler and Fiddle Maker," *Old Time Music* 39 (1984).
9. *Ibid.*
10. Thornton and Emily Spencer, interview conducted by authors in his home, Haw Orchard, VA, October 2016, and Emily Spencer, phone conversation from her home, December 2018.
11. John McCutcheon, phone interview on April 4, 2019.
12. Kilby Spencer, interview with author in his home, 2016.
13. This version of the story is recounted as learned from Albert by Wayne Erbsen, *Hangman's Reel: Dark History and Banjo Tab* (2018), retrieved November 18, 2018, *https://nativeground.com/hangmans-reel-dark-history-banjo-tab/*.

Chapter Notes—Six and Seven

14. Albert Hash, interview with Albert Hash, February 5, 1976, Appalachian State University Libraries Digital Collections, accessed September 6, 2017, *http://omeka.library.appstate.edu/items/show/37314.*
15. Josh Beckworth, *Always Been a Rambler: G.B. Grayson and Henry Whitter, Country Music Pioneers of Southern Appalachia* (Jefferson, NC: McFarland, 2018).
16. Frank Weston, "Albert Hash: Fiddler and Fiddle Maker," *Old Time Music* 39 (1984).
17. Bobby Patterson, interview conducted in Galax, VA, at Bobby's store, The Heritage Shop, shortly before his death in 2017.
18. *Ibid.*

Chapter Six

1. Audrey Hash Ham, interview with Matt Kinman and Martha Spencer, *The Back Porch of America*, no date, retrieved January 7, 2015, *https://www.youtube.com/watch?v=RSjXyaXzzfE.*
2. Randall Eller, interview at Randall's home, Chilhowie, VA, January 17, 2017.
3. Carla Osborne, personal email discussion, January 8, 2018.
4. David Osborne, phone interview, May 14, 2019.
5. Walt Messick, interview at Walt's home, Whitetop Mountain, VA, March 8, 2017.
6. Harold Hensley, personal correspondence to Albert Hash, January 18, 1978.
7. Paul Brown, interview at Paul's home in Raleigh, NC, January 25, 2017.
8. Andy Cahan, interview at Andy's home in Hillsborough, NC, August 18, 2018.
9. Bobby Patterson, interview at The Heritage Shop, Galax, VA, Dec. 18, 2016.
10. *Folkways: Music from the Hills* (aired in 1997), David Holt and Albert Hash, Season 100, Episode 102, 1997, North Carolina Public Broadcasting, *https://www.pbs.org/video/folkways-music-hills/.*
11. Janette Carter, personal correspondence with Albert Hash, October 15, 1978.
12. Brian Grim and Debbie Grim Yates, interview at The Front Porch Gallery, Woodlawn, VA, March 22, 2017.
13. Junior Appalachian Musicians, more information available at *https://jamkids.org.*
14. Wayne Henderson, interview in his guitar shop, November 12, 2016.
15. Mark Sanderford, interview at his home in Martinsville, VA, January 18, 2017.
16. Walt Messick, interview at Walt's home, Whitetop Mountain, VA, March 8, 2017.

Chapter Seven

1. Walt Messick provided us with a verbatim copy of the service he created for Albert.
2. Albert Hash, interview with Albert Hash, February 5, 1976, Appalachian State University Libraries Digital Collections, accessed September 6, 2017, *http://omeka.library.appstate.edu/items/show/37314.*
3. Archie Elmer Powers, interviewed by Edwin Lacy in his home, 2012.
4. Malcolm Gladwell, *Outliers: The Story of Success* (Boston: Little, Brown, 2008).
5. Dean Sturgill, personal interviews with Dean at his home on Spencer Branch, NC, 2016, 2017, 2018.
6. Jerry Smith, personal interview at Jerry's house in Jefferson, NC, 2017.
7. Paul Brown, interview at Paul's home in Raleigh, NC, January 25, 2017.
8. Albert Hash, interview with Edwin Lacy in his Cabin Creek home, 1979.
9. Wilma Testerman, interviewed by Edwin Lacy in her Whitetop, VA, home, 2012.
10. Audrey Hash Ham, interview with Matt Kinman and Martha Spencer, *The Back Porch of America*, no date, retrieved January 7, 2015, *https://www.youtube.com/watch?v=RSjXyaXzzfE.*
11. Carla Osborne, interview in her home in Raleigh, NC, 2017.
12. Brian Grim and Debbie Grim Yates, interview at The Front Porch Gallery, Woodlawn, VA, March 22, 2017.

Chapter Eight

1. J.D. Vance, *Hillbilly Elegy: A Memoir of Family and Culture in Crisis* (New York, HarperCollins, 2016).
2. Albert Hash, interview with Edwin Lacy in his Cabin Creek home, 1979.
3. Loyal Jones, *Appalachian Values* (Ashland, KY: The Jesse Stuart Foundation, 1994).
4. Audrey Hash Ham, *Folkways: The Fiddle*, Public Broadcasting Service, 1999, retrieved April 18, 2019, *https://www.pbs.org/video/folkways-fiddle/*.
5. From a recorded interview found in the Alan Tuillos collection of Albert Hash recordings used by special permission of Kilby Spencer and University of North Carolina.
6. Kevin Donleavy *Strings of Life: Conversations with Old-Time Musicians from Virginia and North Carolina* (Blacksburg, VA, Pocahontas Press, 2004).
7. Personal conversations with Matt Kinman during Johnson County Old Time Fiddlers Convention, Laurel Bloomery, TN, August 2019.
8. Personal interview with Joe Thrift, fiddle maker and musician, at Surry County Community College, May 6, 2019.
9. Chris Testerman's shop, The Mt. Rogers Music Center, can be found on Facebook, *https://www.facebook.com/pg/mountrogersmusiccenter*.

Bibliography

Books

Anderson-Green, Paula H. *A Hotbed of Musicians: Traditional Music in the Upper New River Valley–Whitetop Region*. Knoxville: University of Tennessee Press, 2002.

Beckworth, Josh. *Always Been a Rambler: G.B. Grayson and Henry Whitter, Country Music Pioneers of Southern Appalachia*. Jefferson, NC: McFarland, 2018.

Donleavy, Kevin. *Strings of Life: Conversations with Old-Time Musicians from Virginia and North Carolina*. Blacksburg, VA: Pocahontas Press, 2004.

Eller, Ronald D. *Miners, Millhands, and Mountaineers: Industrialization of the Appalachian South, 1880–1930*. Knoxville: University of Tennessee Press, 1982.

Gladwell, Malcolm. *Outliers: The Story of Success*. Boston: Little, Brown, 2008.

Jones, Loyal. *Appalachian Values*. Ashland, KY: The Jesse Stuart Foundation, 1994.

Ogle, Douglas. *Whitetop: The Great Meadow Mountain of Virginia*. Saltville, VA, 2011.

St. John, Allen. *Clapton's Guitar: Watching Wayne Henderson Build the Perfect Instrument*. New York: Free Press, 2005.

Tannen, Sherree R. *Kenneth Killinger: Mountain Missionary.* Lynchburg, VA: Warwick House, 1995.

Vance, J.D. *Hillbilly Elegy: A Memoir of Family and Culture in Crisis*. New York: HarperCollins, 2016.

Whisnant, David, E. *All That Is Native and Fine*. Chapel Hill: University of North Carolina Press, 1984.

Articles

Spencer, Martha. *Mountain Music Magazine* (2015). Accessed November 7, 2018, https://mountainmusicmagazine.weebly.com/mountain- music-legacies.

Spencer, Thornton. "Fiddlin' Around in the Army." *Mountain Music Magazine* (2013). Retrieved February 11, 2017, *https://mountainmusicmagazine.weebly.com/the-haw-orchard-fiddler.*

Virginia Polytechnic Institute Agricultural Extension Services. *Rural Sociology Report* 64 (March 1948). Retrieved August 30, 2018, https://www.newrivernotes.com/grayson_history_1940_housing_farm.htm.

Weston, Frank. "Albert Hash: Fiddler and Fiddle Maker." *Old Time Music* 39 (1984).

White, Mason. "Elliott, the Tragic Roosevelt." *Hudson Valley Review* 5, no. 1 (1988), 17–29.

Bibliography

Interviews

By Malcolm L. Smith

Brown, Paul. In person, January 2017.
Cohen, Andy. In person, August 2018.
Dowe, Flurry. By Skype, January 2017.
Eller, Randall. In person, January 2017.
Erbsen, Wayne. In person, August 2016.
Fox, Martin. In person, August 2016.
Grim, Brian, and Debbie Grim Yates. In person, March 2017,
Hash, Ernest, Jr. By telephone November 2018.
Hash, Mary Ellen. By telephone, November 2018.
Hash, Rhudy, Jr. By telephone, November 2018.
Henderson, Wayne. In person, November 2016, November 2017, May 2019.
Holt, David. By telephone, April 2019.
Kinman, Matt. In person, August 2018.
McCutcheon, John. By telephone, April 2019.
Messick, Walt. In person, March 2017.
Osborne, Carla. In person, June 2017, and by email, April 2019.
Osborne, David. By telephone, May 2019.
Patterson, Bobby. In person, December 2016.
Rosenbaum, Art. By telephone, April 2019.
Sanderford, Mark. In person, January 2017.
Smith, Jerry. In person, March 2017.
Spencer, Emily, and Thornton Spencer. In person, October 2016.
Spencer, Kilby. In person, November 2016.
Sturgill, Dean. In person, November 2017, May 2018, February 2019.
Thrift, Joe. In person, May 2019.

By Edwin Lacy

Hash, Albert, In person, January 1979.
Powers, Archie Elmer. In person, August 2012.
Testerman, Wilma. In person, August 2012.

Digital Interviews

Hash, Albert. Discussion of Uncle George Finley. *Albert Hash: Vol. 2*. From the collections of Wayne & Max Henderson, the Augusta Heritage Center, and the Spencer family. Field Recorder's Collective CD 707, Track 2, 2015.
Hash, Albert. *Folkways: Music from the Hills*. Season 100, Episode 102, 1997. North Carolina Public Broadcasting. *https://www.pbs.org/video/folkways-music-hills/*.
Hash, Albert. Interview, February 5, 1976. Appalachian State University Libraries Digital Collections, accessed September 6, 2017. http://omeka.library.appstate.edu/items/show/37314.
Ham, Audrey Hash. Interview with Martha Spencer, no date. Accessed November 6, 2018. https://www.youtube.com/watch?v=UZ0TDCUbrBk.
Ham, Audrey Hash. Interview with Matt Kinman and Martha Spencer. *The Back Porch of America*, no date. Retrieved January 7, 2015. *https://www.youtube.com/watch?v=RSjXyaXzzfE*.

Index

Numbers in **_bold italics_** indicate pages with illustrations

Adams, Brian 40
African influence 9, 24
Albert Hash Memorial Band 169
Alden, Ray 9, 104, 123
Appalachian Mountains 3; culture and values 3, 5, 6, 8, 15, 16, 25, 40, 69, 84, 101, 106, 151, 157–162, 169, 175–176; music of 25, 64, 84, 10, 105, 150, 152, 155, 169; red Spruce tree 12, 20, 127–128; settlers 24; women 101
Appalachian State University 39, 54, 145
Appalachian Trail 20
Appalshop 106
"Arkansas Traveler" 12, 34, 45, 112, 178
"The Art of Field Recording" 66, 177; *see also* Rosenbaum, Art

Ball, E.C. (Estil Cortez) 23, 38, 43, 75, 80, 81, 83, 88, 91
Ball, Orna 23, 43, 75, 81
ballads 8, 9, 15, 20, 23, 25, 35, 36, 65, 66, 81, 101, 111, 163, 166, 167
banjo 1, 3, 10, 12, 15, **_18_**, 24, 25, 27, 40, **_45_**, 64, 66, 80, 89, 91–95, 99–101, 104, 109, 110–112, 114, 116, 124, **_125_**, 127, 132, 134–135, 161, 165–166, 167, 170, 173; made by Albert 77
"Barbara Allen" 66, 81
Barr, Tom 112, **_113_**, 124, 126, 127, 166, 172
Barr Haga, Becky **_113_**, 124, 126, 127, 166
bean stringings 9, 24, 39, 160
Beckworth, Josh 108–109, 182n6
Bell, Trudy **_81_**
Berea College, Appalachian Studies 159–160
"Bile Them Cabbage Down" 66, 179
Bill Monroe and His Bluegrass Boys 40

"Black Eyed Susie" 66
"Black Mountain Blues" 66, 102
Blackford family 24
Blevins, Dent 39, 40
Blevins, Frank 12, 40
Blevins, Henry 40
Blevins, Jont 15, 93, 100, 134, 135, 165
Blevins, Nancy 108–109; *see also* "Nancy Blevins"
Blevins, Rebecca 81
bluegrass music 2, 27, 35, 36, 40, 72, 82, 98, 103, **_105_**, 111, 127, 128, 135, 169
The Blue Ridge 4, 7, 12, 20, 24, 41, 42, 92, 145, 152, 155, 157, 173, 174; dancing style 39; music of 24, 26, 109, 125, 130
Blue Ridge Folklife Festival **_149_**
Blue Ridge Music Center 14, 174
Blue Ridge Parkway 174
The Bogtrotters 27
Bramer, Debbie 170
Branch, Jack 172
Bristol, "big bang" of Country Music 9, 24
Bristol sessions 9, 13, 24, 35, 182ch2n17
Brooks, Jim 81
Brown, Paul 103, 104, 114, 123–125, 150, 155, 161, 174
Brunswick Corporation 66–67, 68–71, 78
Burris, Otis 165
Byrd, William 10

Cabin Creek 66–**_67_**, 78, 83–**_84_**, **_98_**, 99, 104, 111, 113, 117, 119, 123, 124, **_129_**, 145, 156, 170, 172, 173
Cabin Creek Instruments 122
"Cabin Home on the Hill" 40
Cahan, Andy 104, 123

189

Index

The Camp Creek Boys 110, 111
Carnegie Hall 2, 82, 85, 88
Carolina Troubadours 40
Carrico, Stuart 100, 101, 102
"The Carroll County Breakdown" 3
The Carroll County Ramblers 27
Carter, A.P. 24, 128
Carter, Janette 128
Carter, Tom 99–100
The Carter Family 112, 128
The Carter Family Fold 24, 128, 150, 168, 170
Carter Mother Maybelle 24
Cherokee tribe 20, 24, 39
cherry bark 8, 28
"Chicken Reel" 8, 46, 178
"Cindy" 66, 179
Civil War 8, 23, 34, 53, 108, 117
Civilian Conservation Corps (CCC) 38–39
Clapton, Eric 71, 72, 87, 88, 148
Clapton's Guitar (St. John) 2
Clinch Valley College 100, 101, 102
"Cluck Old Hen" 66, 179
Cockerham, Fred 64, 109, 110
Colvin, Hiter 111
"Come All Ye Girls" 66
corn 8, 9, 15, 21, 23, 28, 29, 39, 42, 160; husking 9, 24, 38, 39; shucking 9, 38, 39
County Sales 127
The Cowan Creek Music School 169
Cox, Fred 81
Creed, Kyle 110–111, 113–114, 126
"Cricket on the Hearth" 66, 178
"Cripple Creek" 8, 92, 100, 177, 178, 179
Crooked Road Music Trail 173
Crooked Road Ramblers 166
"Cumberland Gap" 66, 178, 179
Cunningham, Jackson 163–164

dances *see* mountain dancing
"Dark Haired Girl" 66
"Darling True Love" 66
Dartmouth 123
Davis and Elkins 123
Davis, Luther 103, 125
Dickens, Hazel 123
Dixie Serenaders 12
"Don't Let Your Deal Go Down" 66
Dowe, Flurry 91–95, 97–98, 99, 101–102, 110, 111, 112, **113**, 114, 121, **125**, 134, 161, 165
Dr Pepper 5, 91, 96, 111

"Dugannon" 112
dulcimer 117, ***120***, 121–122, 141, 163, 171–172
"dumb bull" 31
Dunford, Eck 24, 27
Duvall, Bruce 30–31

East, Earnest 124
Edmonds, "Uncle" Norman 24, 65, 125
Eller, Randall 116–118, 150, 172
England 9, 14, 20, 79, 87, 161, 173
Erbsen, Wayne 104, 183*ch*4*n*13

Faith Lutheran Church ***143***
Farmer, Gaither 38
Ferrum College 123, ***149***
fiddle 1, 4, 5, 7–8, 10, 12, 13–14, 23, 24, 25, 29–30, 32, 33, 34, 36, 38, 39, 40, 44, 45, ***60***, 62–63, 65, 75, 76–77, 78, 80, 84, 89, 9, 94, 95, 99, 102, 107, 108, 110–112, 122, 123, 132, 133, 135, 138–139, 152, 155, 160–161, 163, 167, 170–***176***; Albert's exchange of for birth of Audrey 42–43; Albert's first building of 16–19, 21; Albert's first hearing of 15; Albert's style of playing 102–104; bow 14, 15, 16, 17, 18, 19, 34, 45, 73, 92, 9, 107, 135, 165; bowing styles 14, 34, 62, 65, 104, 133, 135, 161; festivals and contests 9, 10, 13, 24, 25, 31, 102, 104, 112, 114, 121, 123, 124, 127, 134, 135, 138, 146, 150, 165, 166, 168; making of 12, 16–19, 53, 54, 56–***59***, 66, 68, 76, 79, 83, 98, 100, 115–119, 123, 125–127, 127–128, 157, 158, 159, 166; Thornton's learning of 46–47; tunes 8, 20, 40, 92, 108–110, 112, 157, 164–165
"The Fiddler of Fees Branch" (Sturgill, Dean) 44–45
The Field Recorder's Collective 104, 15, 161, 173, 177, 182*n*23
Finlay, Archie 40
Finley, George 8, 14, 16, 23, 30, 33–34, 103, 152
"Flop Eared Mule" 66, 178
Floyd Old Time Gathering 169
Folkways (PBS) 127, 163, 184*ch*6*n*10
Fort Benning (Georgia) 62–63
Fox, Martin 47, 92–95, 95–98, 99, 101, 106
France 20
Fry, Joshua 10

Galax Old Fiddler's Convention 26–27, 75, 166

190

Index

Gaultney, Muncie 165
Gentry, Johnny 166
Gentry, Nancy 166
Germany 21, 24
Gerrard, Alice 104, 123
Gid Tanner and the Skillet Lickers 8, 23
ginseng 8, 28
Gobble, Sam 126
grandfather clock 1, 53–55, 126
Grayson, Gilliam Banmon or G.B. 8, 13, 34, 35–36, 103, 125; *see also* Grayson and Whitter
Grayson and Whitter 8, 13, 23, 34, 35, 36, 108
Great Depression 25, 27, 29, 31, 159
"The Great Physician" 66, 178
"Green Valley Waltz" 112
Greer, Smith 81, 144
Grim, Brian 104, 133, 134, *135*, *136*, *137*, 141, 152
Grim, Lorene 133
Grim Yates, Debbie 134, *135*, *136*, *137*, 141, 152
guitar 5, 7, 12, 14, 15, 23, 25, 27, 31, 35, 40, 46, 58, 60, *61*, 62–63, 80, 82, 83, 85, 86, 89, 95, 99, 100, 118, 124, 132, 133, 134, 138, 147–148, 166, 167, 170, 173; Henderson made 1–2, 4, 72, *73*, 75, 76–77, 85, *87*, 99, 161, 170, 172, 173; introduction into mountain music 25, 30; made by Albert 4, 77–78, *79*; making 4; played by Emily Spencer 102, 110, 112; played by Thornton Spencer 94, 100, 110, 165; playing machine 33
The Gully Jumpers 75
gunsmithing 43, 48, 55, 120, 148
Guthrie, Woody 27

Haire, Rector 81
"Handsome Molly" 36, 66, 178
"Hangman's Reel" 4, 106–108, 111, 151, 174, 184*ch*4*n*13
harmonica 10, 35, 111
Hart, Dean 40, 81
Hash, Abraham Lincoln 15, 20, *22–23*, 29, *30*
Hash, Audrey 2, 4, *42*, 43, 53, 66, 73–74, 81, 115–*117*, 118, 119, *120*, 122–123, 130–132, 138, 147, 152, 153, 162–164, 168, 171, 172, 173
Hash, Benjamin 108
Hash, Dennis 15, 17, 27, *28*
Hash, Ernest 7, 15, 27–*28*, 31, 40
Hash, Ethel *26*, 39–46, 48, 52, 53, *56*, 62, 65, 66, *74*, 83–84, 89, 95, *96*, *98*, 118, 119, 120, 121, 123, 128, 129, 130, 139, 142, 147, 159, 160
Hash, Joyce Mae *42*, 43, 52, 73, 119–120, *124*
Hash, Rhudy 7, 15, 27, 40, 46
Haw Orchard Cemetery 5, 91, 157, 167, 170
Hazel and Alice 123
Henderson, Max 1, 80, *81*, 82, 84, 98, 99
Henderson, Walter 1, 23, 75
Henderson, Wayne 1–2, 4, 5, 23, 72-, *87*, 128, 138, 147, 152, 161, 170, 172, 173
Hensley, Harold 122–123
Heritage Records 127, 165, 177
Hill, Lon 40
The Hill Billies 24
"hillbilly" 6, 64, 145, 158; music 9, 13, 24, 34, 35
Holt, David 5, 104, 127–128, 163, 184*ch*6*n*10

"I Never Will Marry" 112
"Interstate Music Festivals on Whitetop Mountain" *see* Whitetop Mountain, Interstate Music Festivals on)
Ireland 8, 9, 20, 24, 104
"I've Always Been a Rambler" 36, 178

Jarrell, Ben 24
Jarrell, Tommy 24, 64, 103, 104, 109, 110, 111, 125, 150
Jefferson, Peter 10–11
Jefferson, Thomas 11
"Jenny Put the Kettle On" 12
"John Henry" 66
"Johnson Boys" 8, 178
"Johnson's Old Grey Mule" 66, 178
Jones, Baldwin 100
Jones, Loyal 159–160
Junior Appalachian Musicians (JAM) 138, 148, 184*n*13

Kansas 4
Kemp, J.C. 80, 81
Kentucky 7, 106, 109, 123, 138, 160; Whitesburg 106, 169
Kinman, Matt 171–172
Konnarock Critters 133–*136*, *137*, 152
Konnarock Kritters *see* Konnarock Critters

Lacy, Casey 3
Lacy, Edwin 3, 57, 188

191

Index

Lewis, Dr. Helen 101
"Little Brown Hand" *see* "Took Her By the Little Brown Hand
"Little Log Cabin in the Lane" 66
Lomax, Alan 9, 65, 75
"Lonesome Road Blues" 13
Long, Emmet 15, 27, 93
Long Reedy, Della Mae 15, 20, 22, 23, 29, *30*, 32–33, *56*, 65–66
"Lost John" 111, 178
Lundy, Emmett 27, 103, 125

Martin Guitars 40, 75, 77
"Masters of the Steel String Guitar" tour 82
McClennan, Cindy 92, 93, 95, 99, 101, 106
McCutcheon, John 5, 104–105, 107–108
Messick 121–122, 141, 143–156, 172
Milan, Italy 107
Montgomery, Alabama 92, 97
Montgomery and Ward 25
The Moonlight Ramblers 12
Mt. Rogers 20, 158; fire station 131, *133*
Mt. Rogers High School 8, 23, 25, 29, 33, 38, 39, 130, *132*
Mountain City Fiddler's Convention 35
mountain dancing 10, 14, 15, 18, 20, 24–26, 34, 38, 39, 45, 76, 80, 86, 94, 102, 108, 109, 134, 138, 152, 160, 170; "buck and wing" 25; flatfooting 25, 128, 141, 166
Mountain Dew 64, 138
Mountain Records 110–111, 126, 177
"My Child Is Gonna Be a Minor" 112

"Nancy Blevins" 100, 108–109, 151, 174, 177, 179
Nashville 9, 13, 92, 171
National Endowment for the Humanities (NEH) 99
New Hampshire 4, 123
New River 7, 35
New River Festival 112
"New River Train" 13
New York 9, 11, 13, 20, 35, 64, 65, 104, 123, 124, 168
New York Times 72
North Carolina 8, 10, 20, 24, 40, 43, 110, 123, 125, 138, 165, 166, 174; Ashe County 40, 89, 108; Asheville 169; Boone 83; Crumpler 36, 108; Deep Gap 82; Fees Branch 8, 15, 29, 31, 39, 41, 42, 43, 44–45, 47–48, 74, 119, 130, 145; Fees Gap 29; Healing Springs *37*; Jefferson 27, 42, 140, 143, 174; Lansing 1, 12, 50, 75, 145; Mt. Airy 24, 124; Surry County 109; Union Grove 65; West Jefferson 115; Wilkesboro 82
Northcutt, Bill 106

"Old Joe Clark" 8, 178, 179
"Old Originals" 100, 177
"Old Sport" 106, 111, 151, 188, 179
The Old-Time Herald 4
"Omie Wise" 64, 66, 177, 178
Osborne, Carla 119–120
Osborne, David 120, 129, *131*, 153
Outliers (Gladwell, Malcolm) 148
Owen, Blanton 9, 99, 102, 188

Paisley, Brad 72
Patterson, Bobby 110, 111, 125–126, 165
Peer, Ralph 35
Phoenix Mountain 7
The Pine Ridge Boys 111, 124
Poe, Jim 40, 80, *81*
Poole, Barbara 167
Poverty Gulch Band 112
Powers, Archie 47, 163, 173
Puckett, Riley 165

"Rabbit Up a Gump Stump" 66, 111, 178
radio 9, 3, 150, 155; Albert Hash on 1, 31, 80–*81*, 98, 167, 174; influence on country music 9, 63–64
Radio Bristol 167
"Ragtime Annie" 40, 46, 63, 66, 178
Rector, John 24
The Red Hots 173
Reed, Ola Belle 165
Reedy, Blair 80
Reedy, Bobby 81, 108, 134
Reedy, Gary 81
Reedy, Jack 12
Reedy, Jim 108
Reedy, Thomas 30, 120
Reedy, Wayne 38
"Reel du Pendu" 106
Ringling Bros. Circus 15, 27
Roosevelt, Eleanor 7, 10, 11, 20, 26
Roosevelt, Elliott 11–12
Roosevelt, Theodore 11
The Rose Bowl Parade 169
"Rose Connelly" 66
Rosenbaum, Art 9, 64–66
Rounder Records 99–100, 177

Index

"Sally Goodin" 15, 178, 179
Scotland 8, 20
Sears and Roebuck 25
Seeger, Charles 9
Seeger, Mike 9
Seeger, Pete 9
Seeger, Ruth 9
Sharp, Cecil 9
Sheets, Joe 165
Shelor family 24
"Short Life of Trouble" 36
Sigmon, Larry 167
Sing Out! 4
"Single Girl" 112
Smedley the turkey 86
Smith, Arthur 8, 23, 103, 111, 125
Smith, Jerry 51, 55, 60–*61*, 62, *81*, 87–88, 149, 154
Smithsonian Institute 9, 14, 19, 31, 82, 142, 146, 163, 173; National Folklife Festival of 123, 168
"Soldier's Joy" 66, 178
Spencer, Emily Paxton 4, 5, *94*, 100–103, 110–*113*, 126–127, 130, 132, 134, 135, 137–138, 154, 156, 162, 165–167, 168–170
Spencer, Martha 166–167, 170, 171
Spencer, Orie Lance 39, *96*
Spencer, Paul 100
Spencer, Thornton 5, 26, 46–47, 62–63, 64, 86, 89–91, 92–*94*, *96*–99, 100–102, 106, 110, 111–114, 119, 121, 122, *125*, 126–127, 130, 131, 132, 133, 134, 135, 138, 154, 156, 161, *164*–168, *169*, 170, 173
Spencer, "Uncle" Bud *26*, 39, 182*n*3
Spencer, Zollie Mae *96*
"Spencer Branch" 166
Spencer's Trading Post 89, 92, *94*, 104, 111
Sprague Electric 48, 50–52, 53, 55, 57, 60–61, 65, 66, 68, 70, 77, 87, 149
Stamper, Corbett 8, 15, 16, 23, 24, 30, 93, 100, 101, 151, 165
Stoneman, Earnest 24
Stoneman Family 24
"The Storms Are on the Ocean" 112
Strings of Life (Donleavy, Kevin) 165, 182*n*5
Sturgill, Breece 43–44
Sturgill, Dave 173
Sturgill, Dean 5, 31, 43, 44–47, 89, 91, 93, 149, 161, 182*n*12
Sturgill, Johnny 112

Tannen, Sheree 21
Tennessee 8, 10, 35, 36, 109, 111, 138; Bristol 36; Jonesborough 7; Kingsport 92; Knoxville 138, 142; Konnarock 12, 20, 121, 131, 133; Laurel Bloomery 36
Testerman, Chris 150, 163–164, 173, 185n9
Things I Left Behind (Spencer, Thornton) 167
Thrift, Joe 5, 104, 173
timber companies 10, 11, 21
"Tom Dooley" 36, 66
"Took Her by the Little Brown Hand" 66, 111, 178
"Train 45," 66, 177, 179
Traynham, Jenny 104
Traynham, Mac 104

"Uncle Joe" 8, 178
"The Unique Sound of the Mountains" 167
University of Virginia 100

Victrola 8, 23, 30, 36, 63
Virginia 7–8, 10, 11, 12, 24, 27, 36, 42, 43, 47, 65, 66, 85, 89, 100, 101, 106, 117, 119, 123, 127, 134, 138, 150, 154, 162, 165, 166, 169, 173, 174; Abingdon 11; Appomattox 46; Arlington 40, *41*, 100; Baywood 39; Big Stone Gap 169; Bristol 7, 12, 172; Carroll County 99, 111; Chilhowie 172; Damascus 36; East Radford 12; Elk Creek 23; Fancy Gap 170; Ferrum 123, *149*; Floyd 127, 169; Floyd County 3, 99; Franklin County 99; Fries 13, 24, 35, 155; Galax 20, 24, 27, 92, 103, 109, 110, 112, 123, 124, 125, 126, *140*, 143, 166, 170, 172; General Assembly of 8, 142–143; Grayson County 2, 3, 4, 5, 7, 8, 20, 21, 23, 24, 27, 31, 35, 66, 99, 155; Grayson Highlands Region 8, 20, 66; Haw Orchard *169*; Hillsville 65; Hiltons 128; Independence 97, 100; Marion 36; Patrick County 99; Rugby 20, 23, 72, 73, 75, 78, 82, 85, *87*, 99; Sugar Grove 66; Taylor's Valley 40; Whitetop 4, 7, *67*, 143, 173; Wytheville 3
Virginia Carolina Boys *81*–83, 98, 177
Virginia Creeper railway 21, 181
Virginia Folklife Festival 123, *149*
Virginia Supply 29
Virginia Tech 134

"Wabash Cannonball" 40
wagon train 82

193

Index

The Waltons 122–123
Ward, Wade 24, 64, 109
Washington, George 11
Washington, D.C. 9, 31, 40, 123, 146, 150, 173
Washington Mill 35
Watson, Doc (Arthel Lane) 2, 64, 72, 82–83, 98, 166
"Way Over in the Promised Land" 19
Weston, Frank 30, 181*n*10
West Virginia 7, 123; Elkins 102
"Whisperin' Winds" 113
Whitetop Jiggers 12
Whitetop Mountain 4, 7–13, 20, 34, 36, 93, 106, 120, 127, 129, 134, 139, 152, 157; Interstate Folk Festivals on 12–14, 24–**26**, 27
Whitetop Mountain Band 4, 39–40, 46, 94, 108, 112–114, 120, 123, 126–128, 134, 138, 141, 152, 166–170

Whitetop Mountain Boys 110, 112
Whitter, Henry 13, 24, 34–**37**, 108–109, 111, 181*ch*1*n*6
"Who's Calling You Sweetheart Now" 66
Wild Goose Uprising 3
Wilkes Community College 102, 142
"Will You Be Loving Another Man" 40
Wilson, Clay 40
Winebarger's Mill 165, 177
WKSK Radio, West Jefferson, NC 80–82
Wolf Knob School 29, 31
Wolf Trap National Center for the Performing Arts 123
World War II 23, 31, 50, 160
World's Fair, 1982 31, 138–139, 142, 145, **175**
"The Wreck of the Old Southern 97" 13, 35

Yates, John 40

www.ingramcontent.com/pod-product-compliance
Ingram Content Group UK Ltd.
Pitfield, Milton Keynes, MK11 3LW, UK
UKHW042008140426
5217IPUK00015B/1059